CRAZY COLORING BOOK

&

MYSTIC FOREST OF CHI

COLORING BOOK

CRAZY

Coloring Book For Adults

AMAZINGLY RELAXING INSANITY

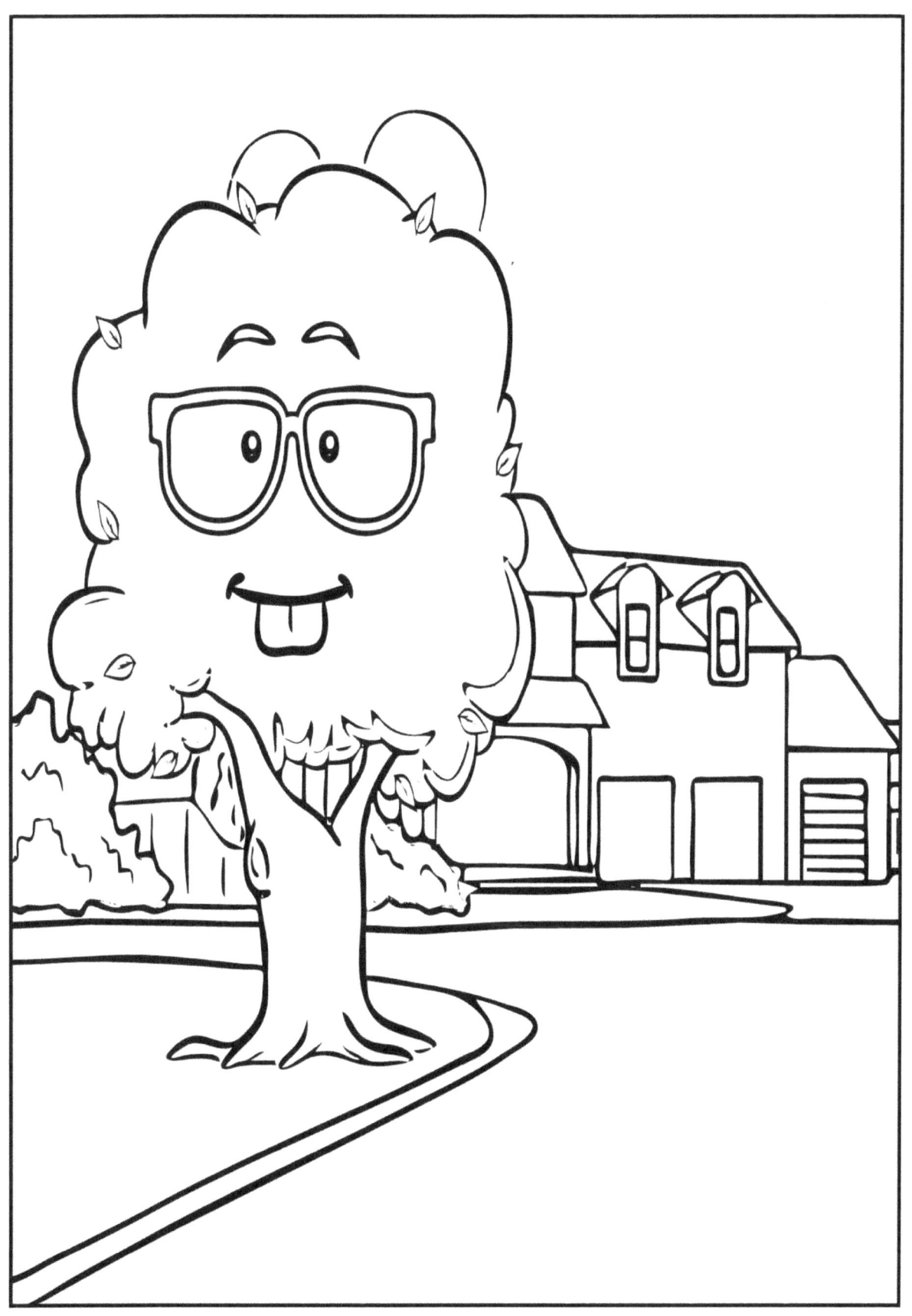

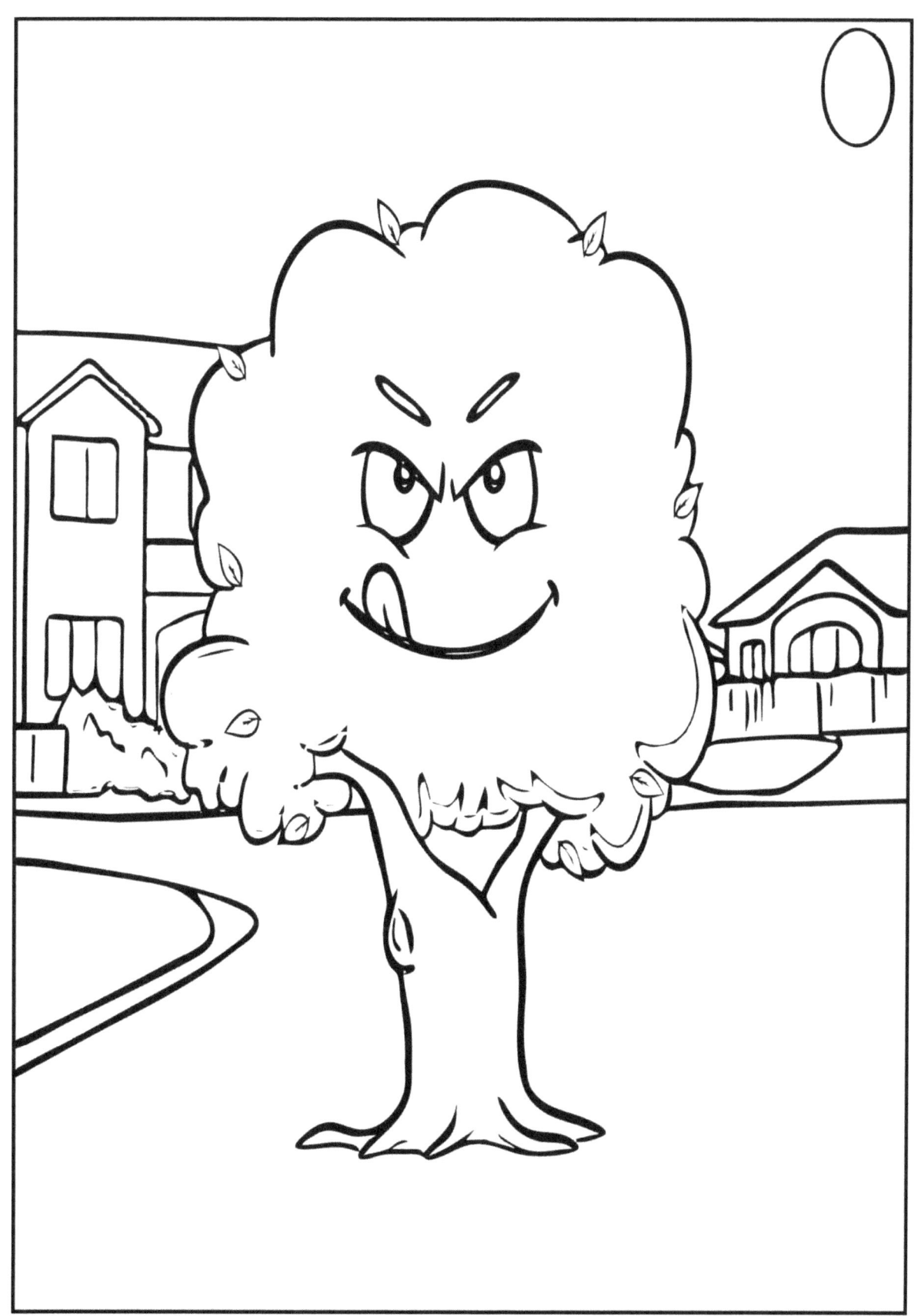

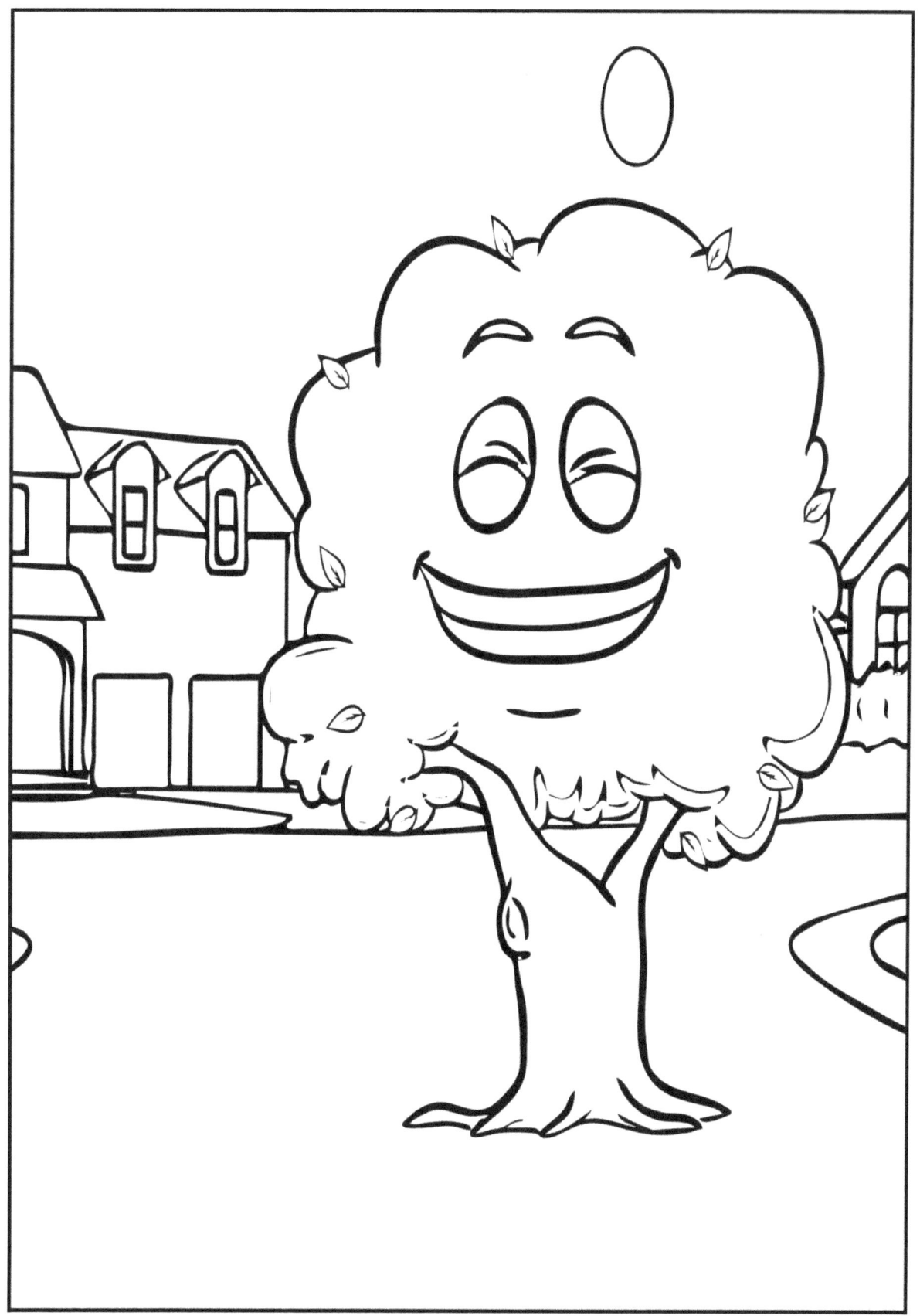

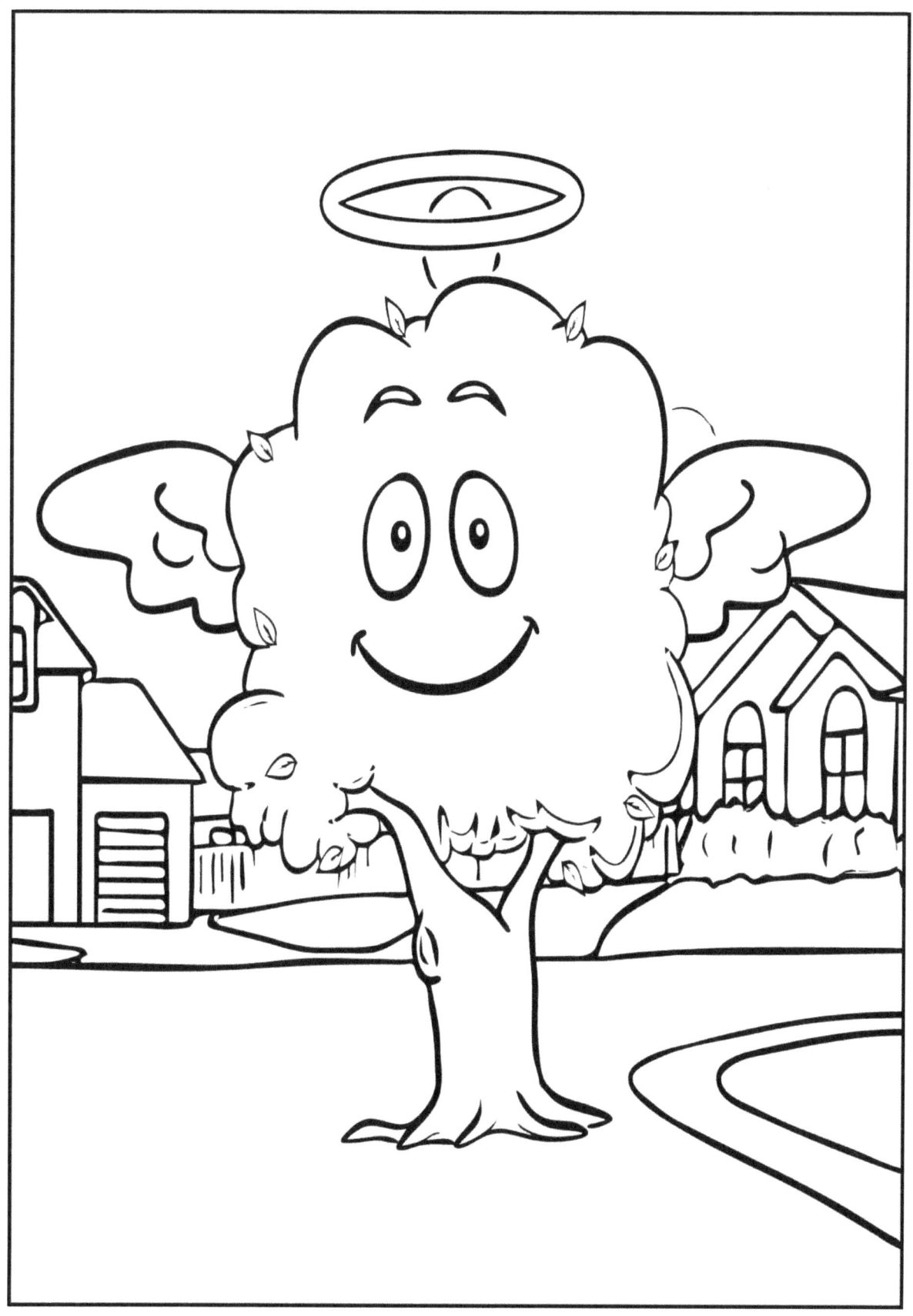

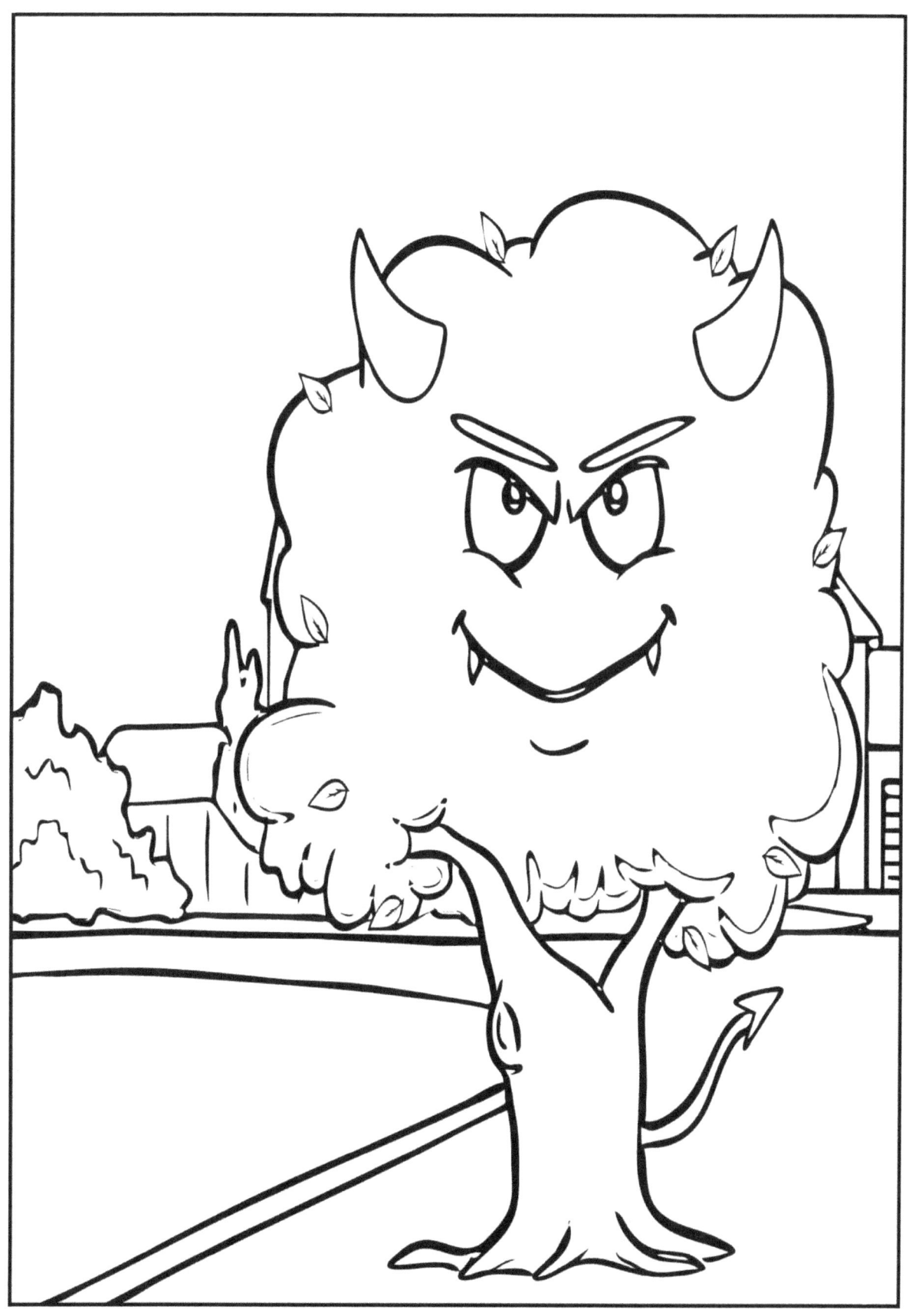

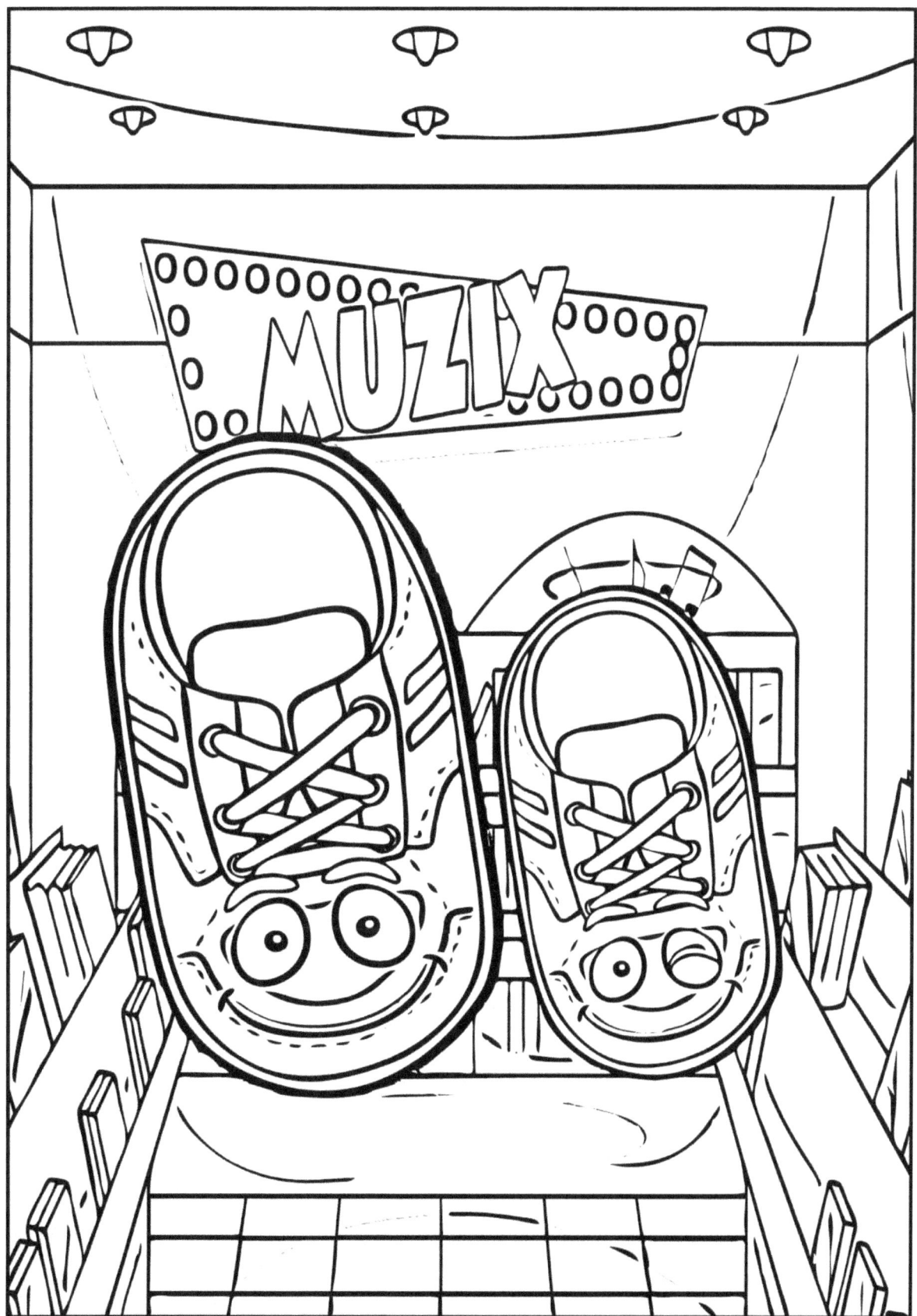

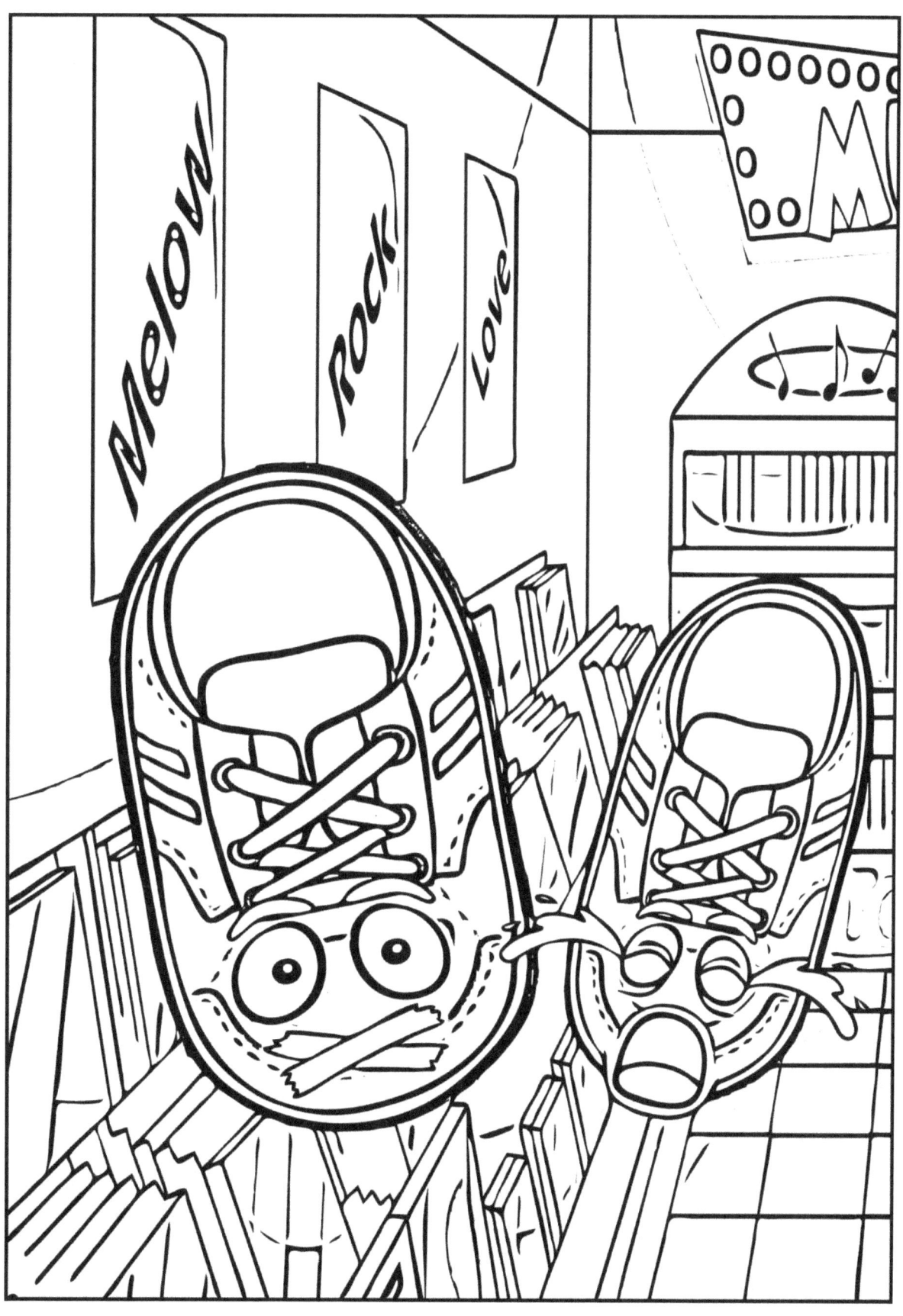

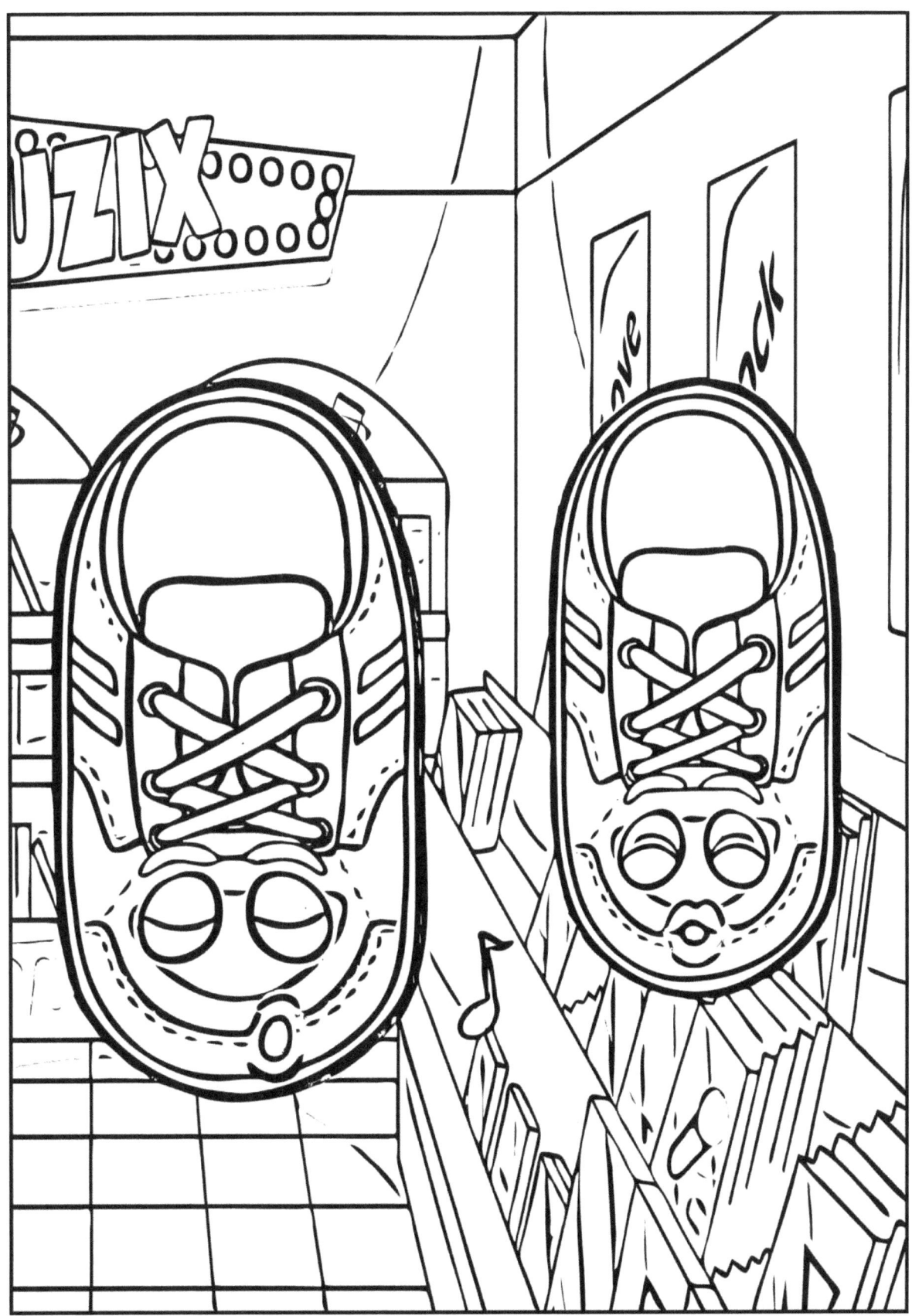

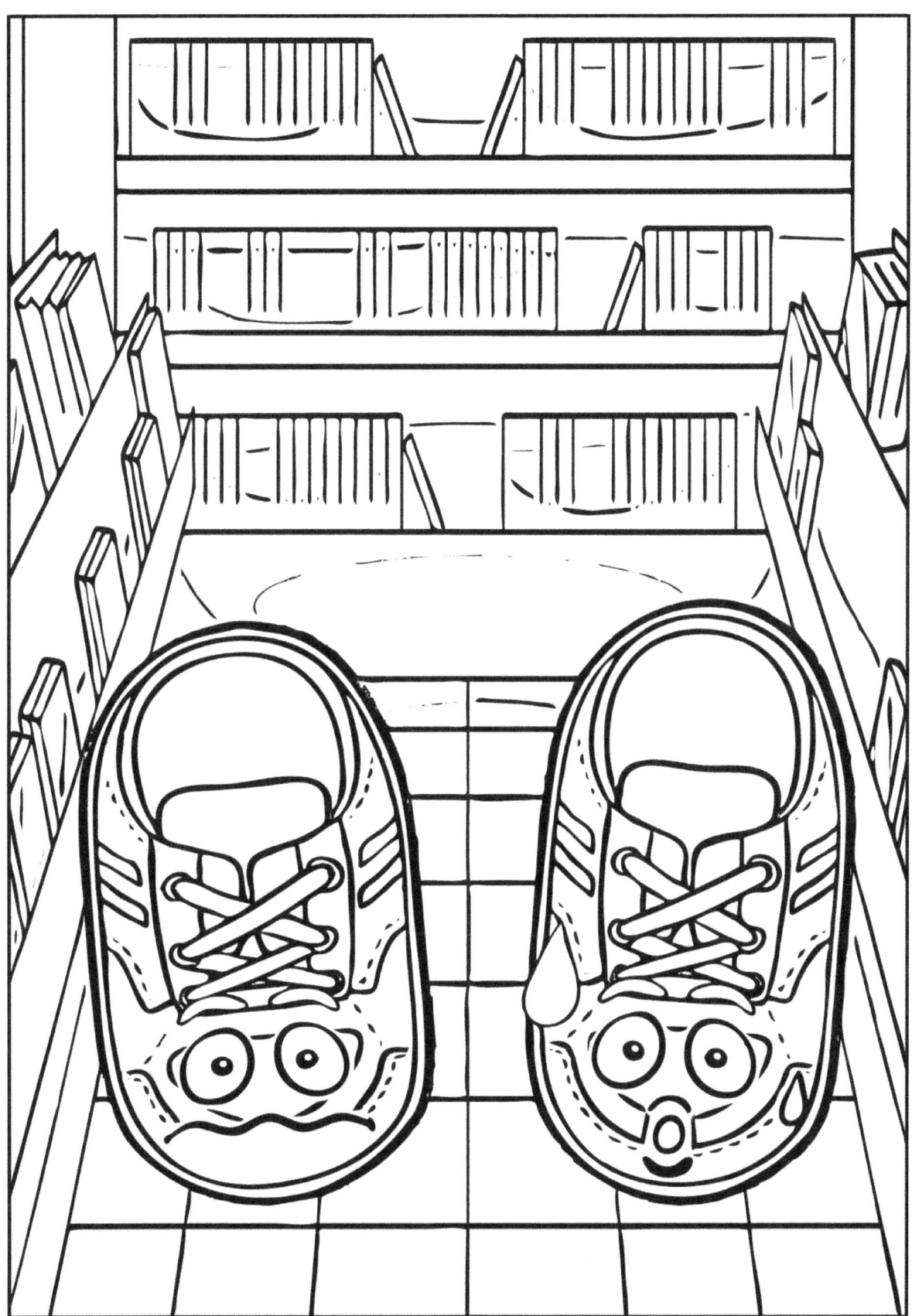

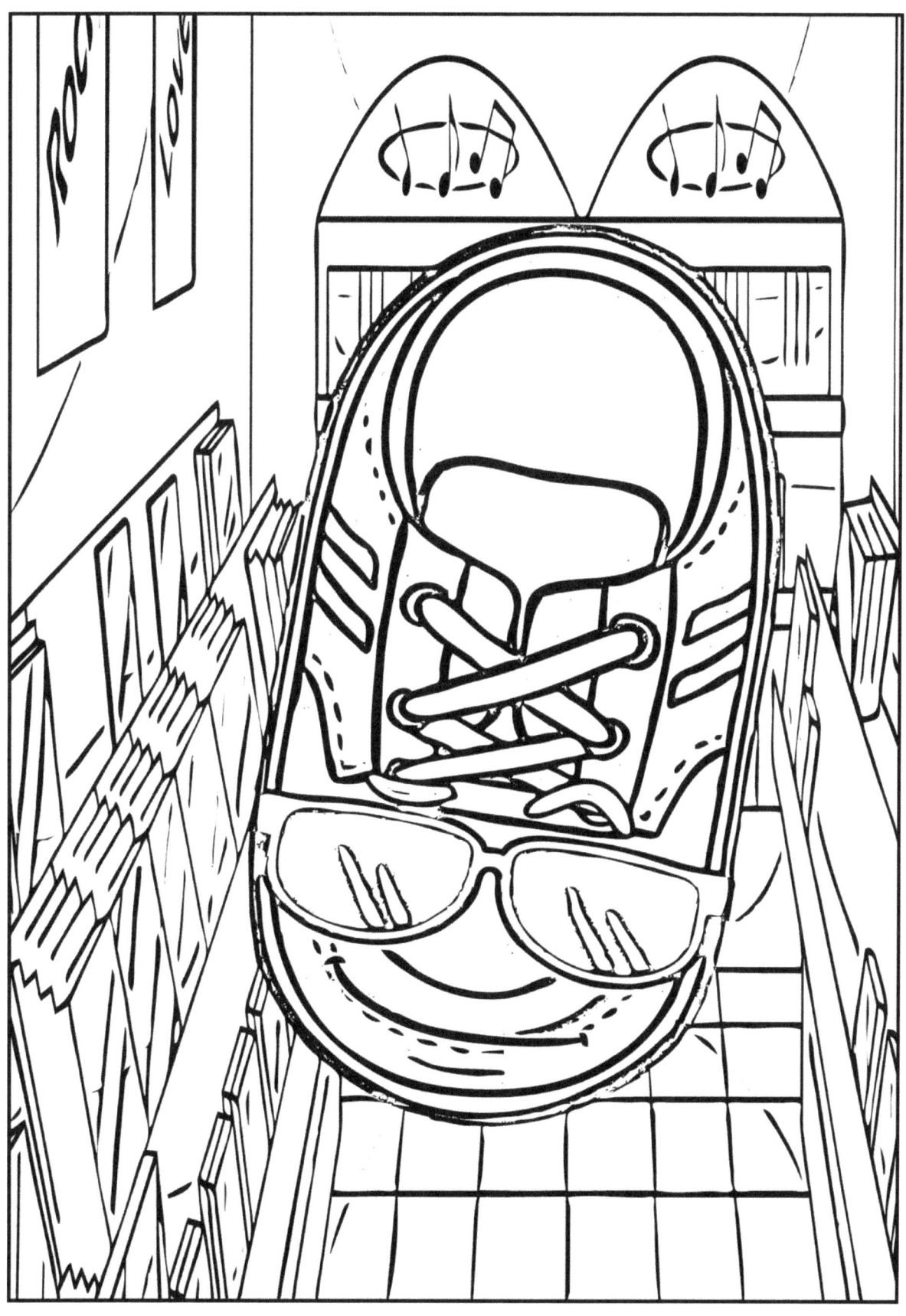

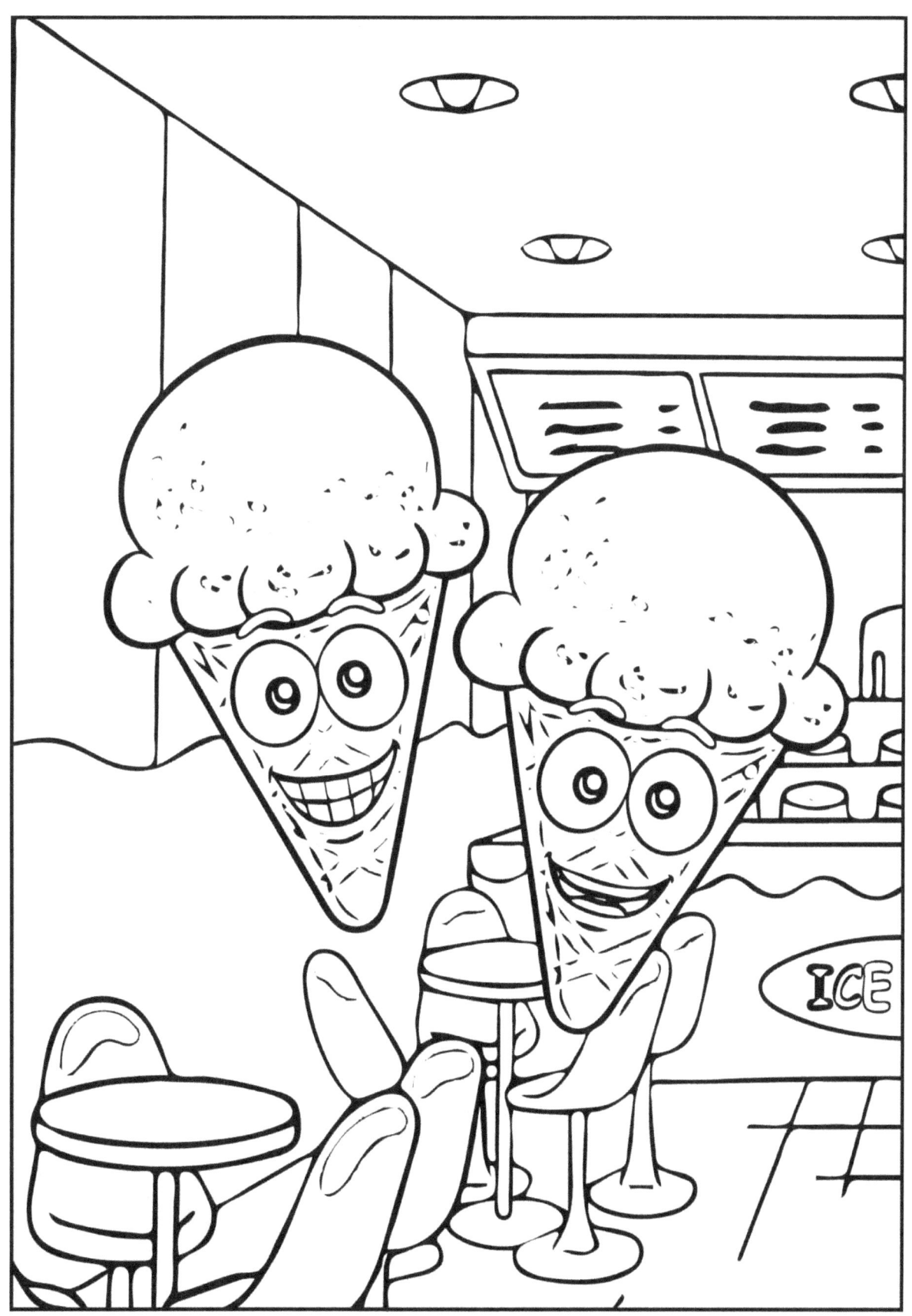

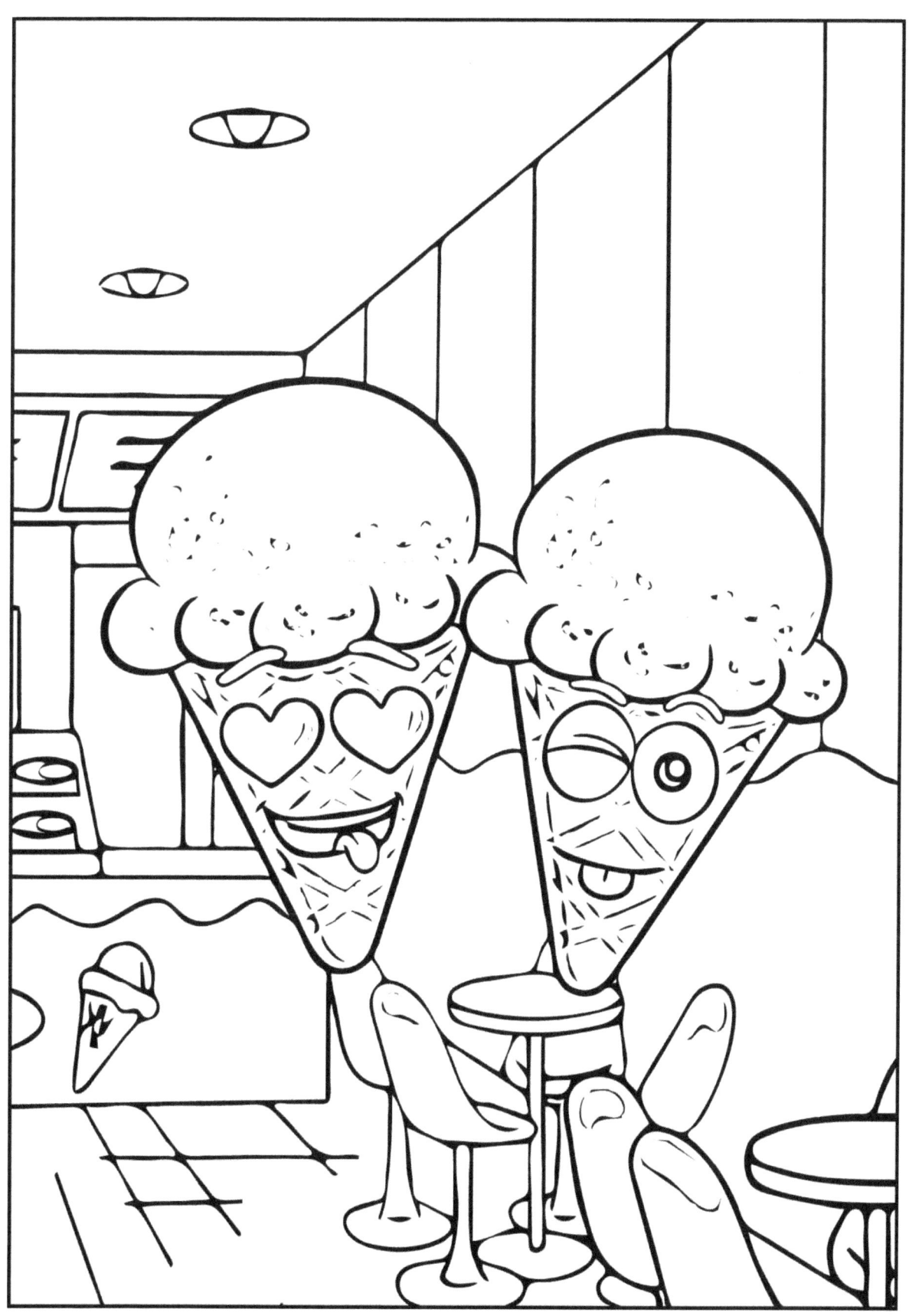

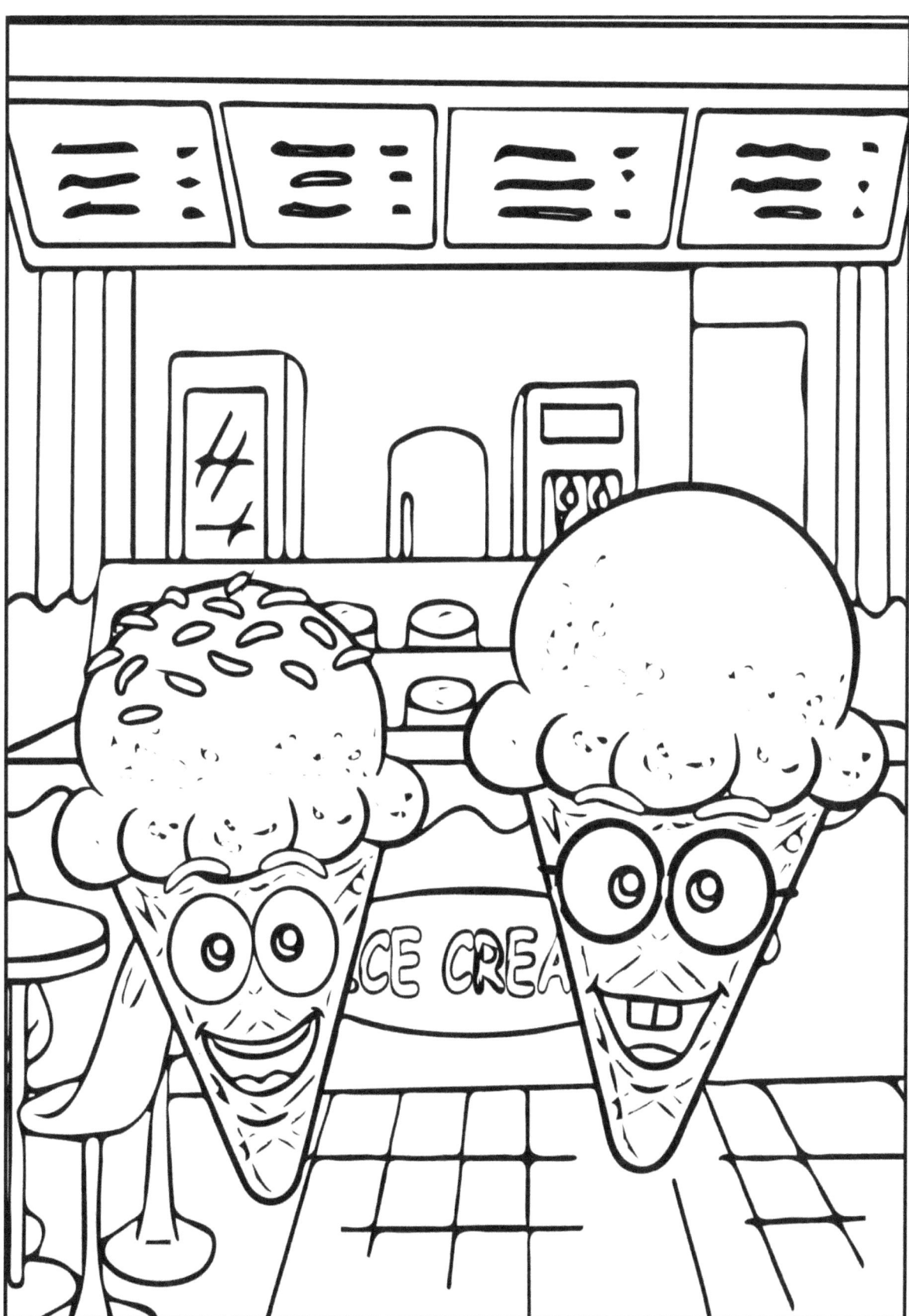

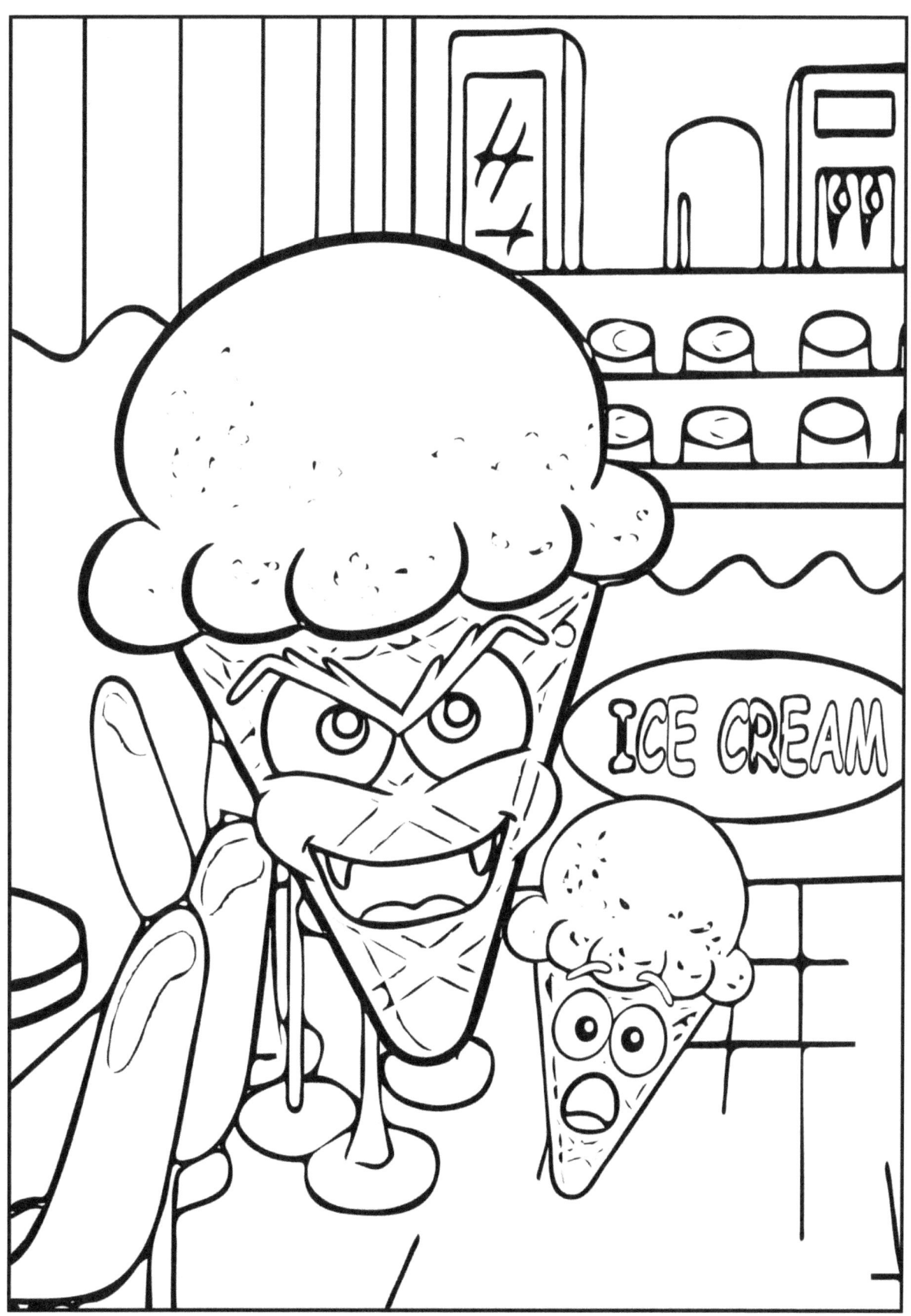

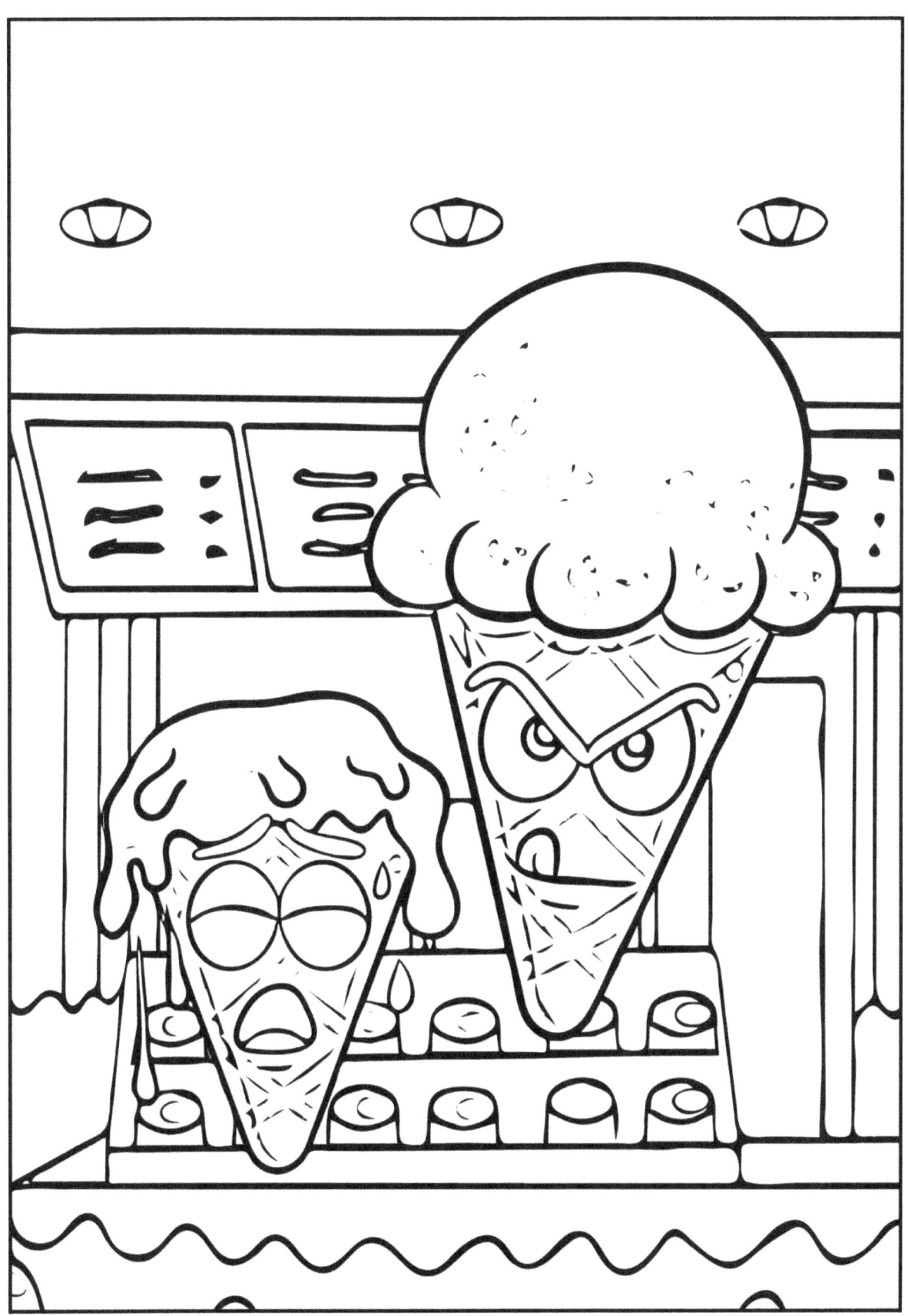

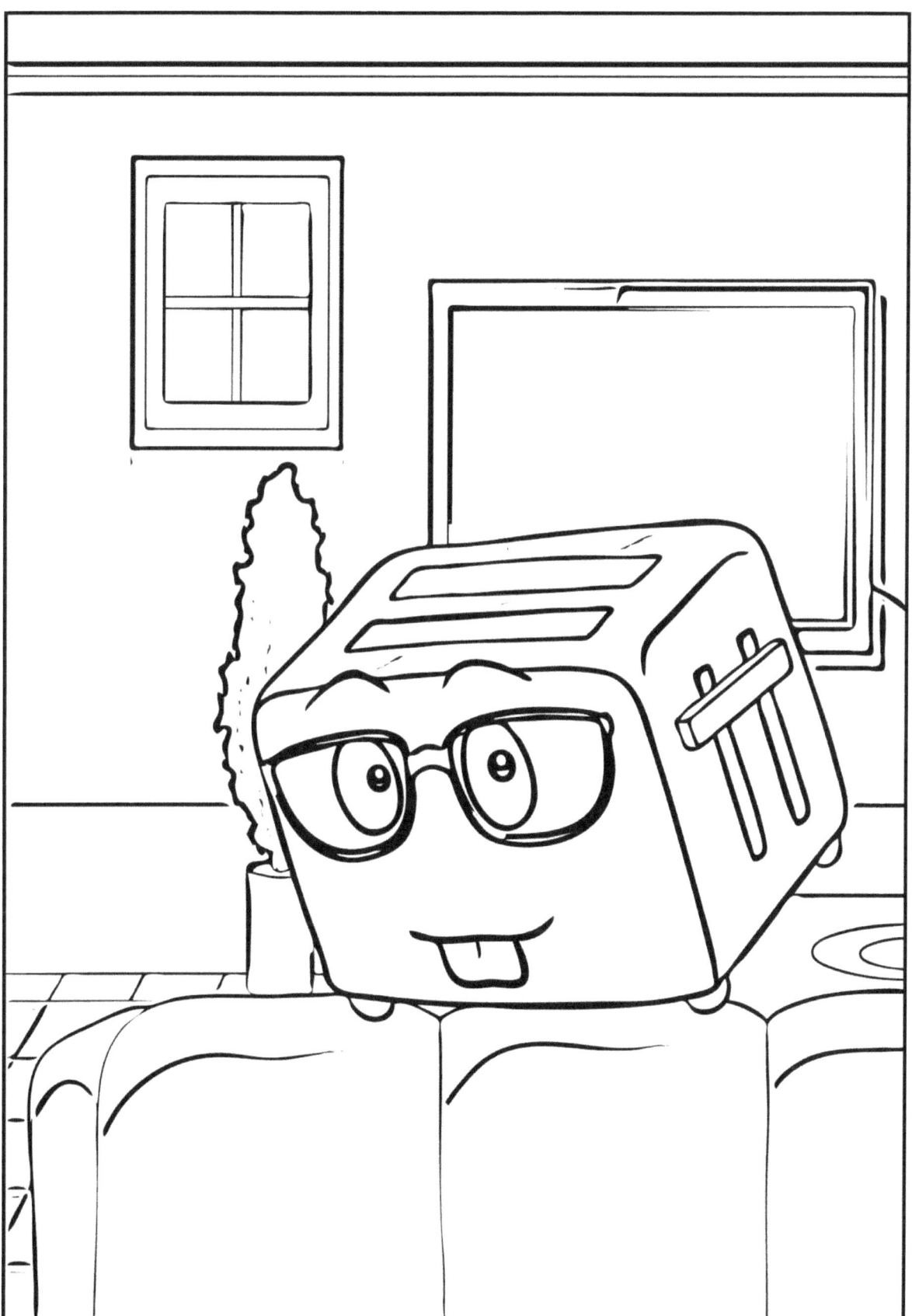

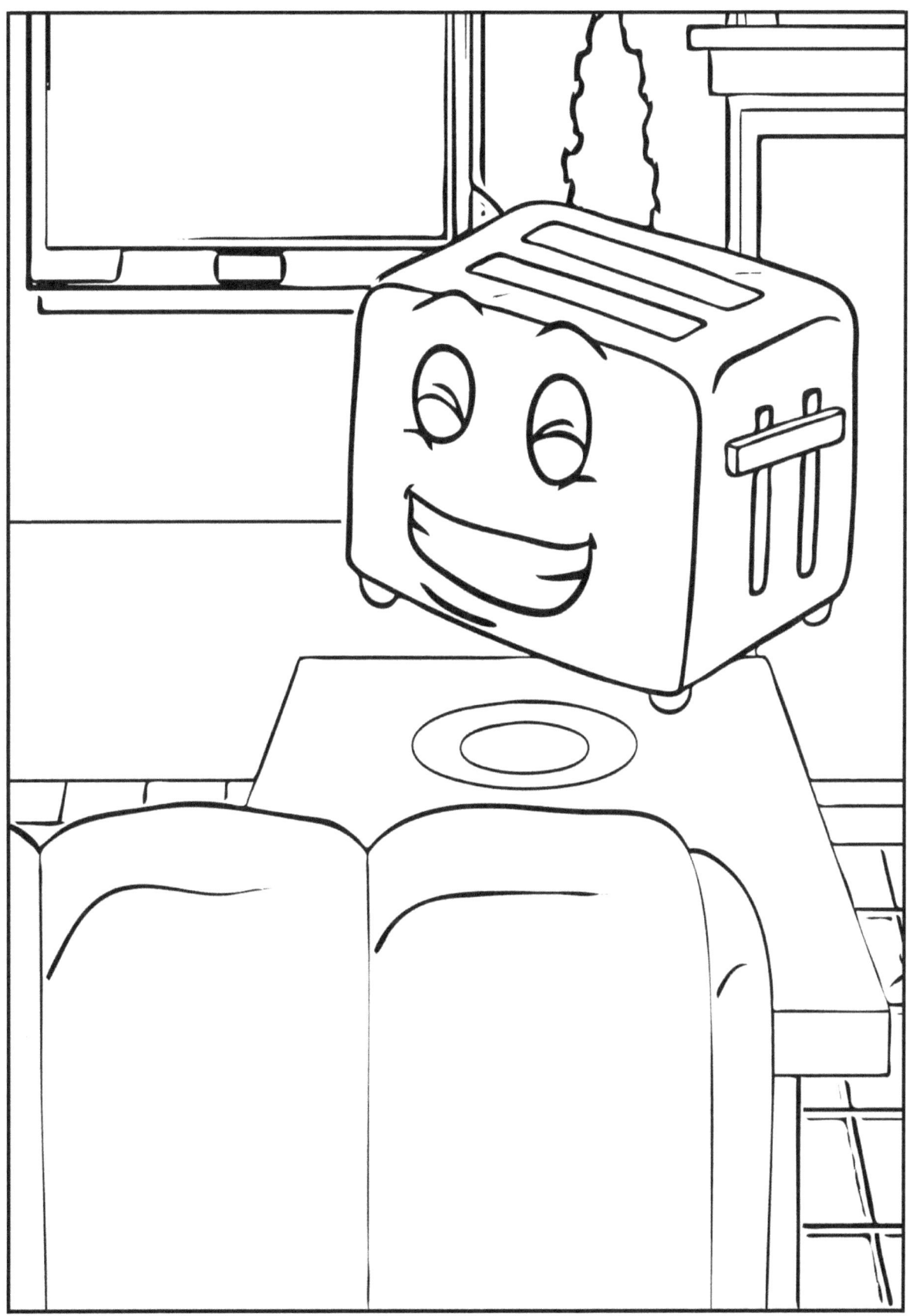

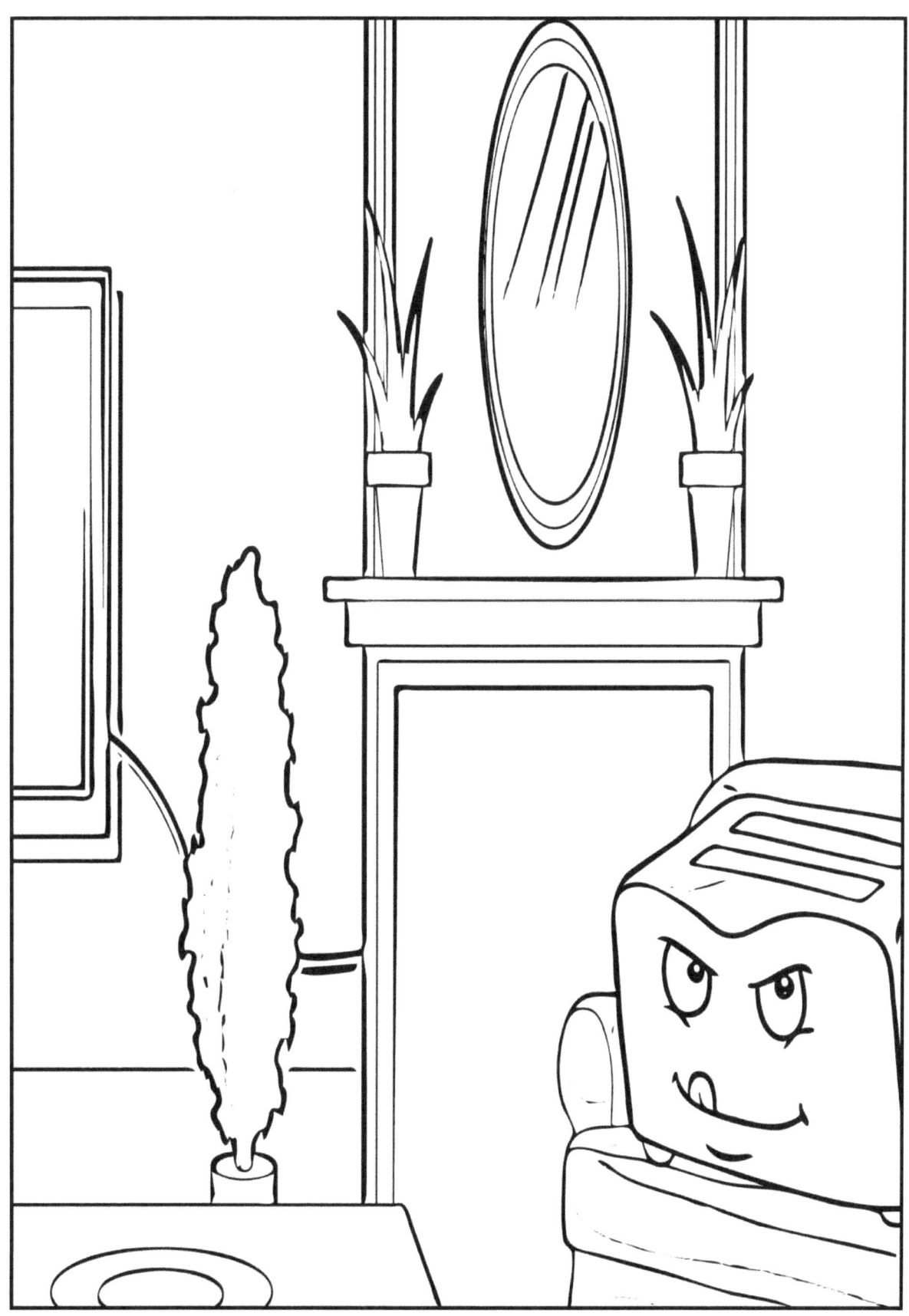

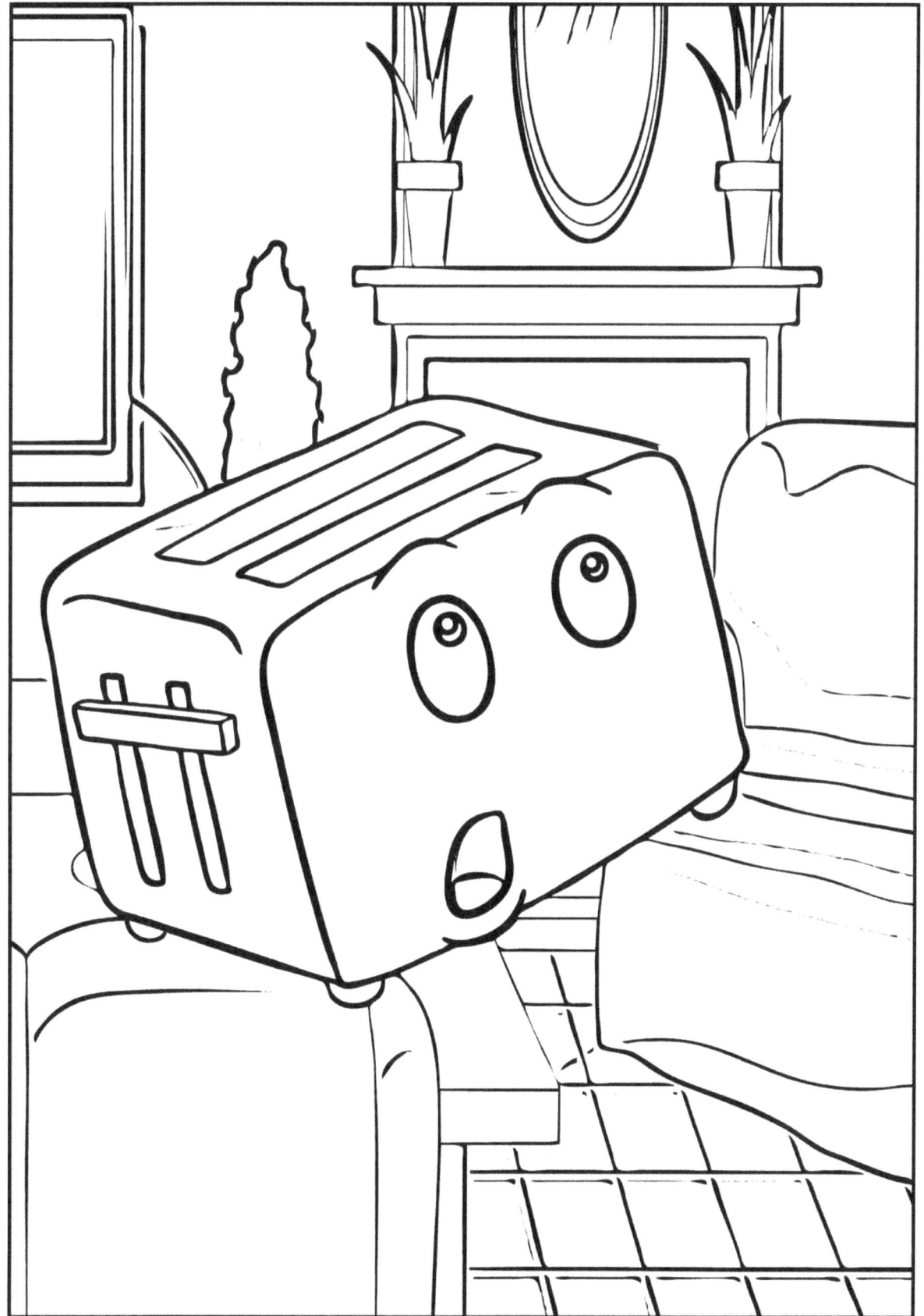

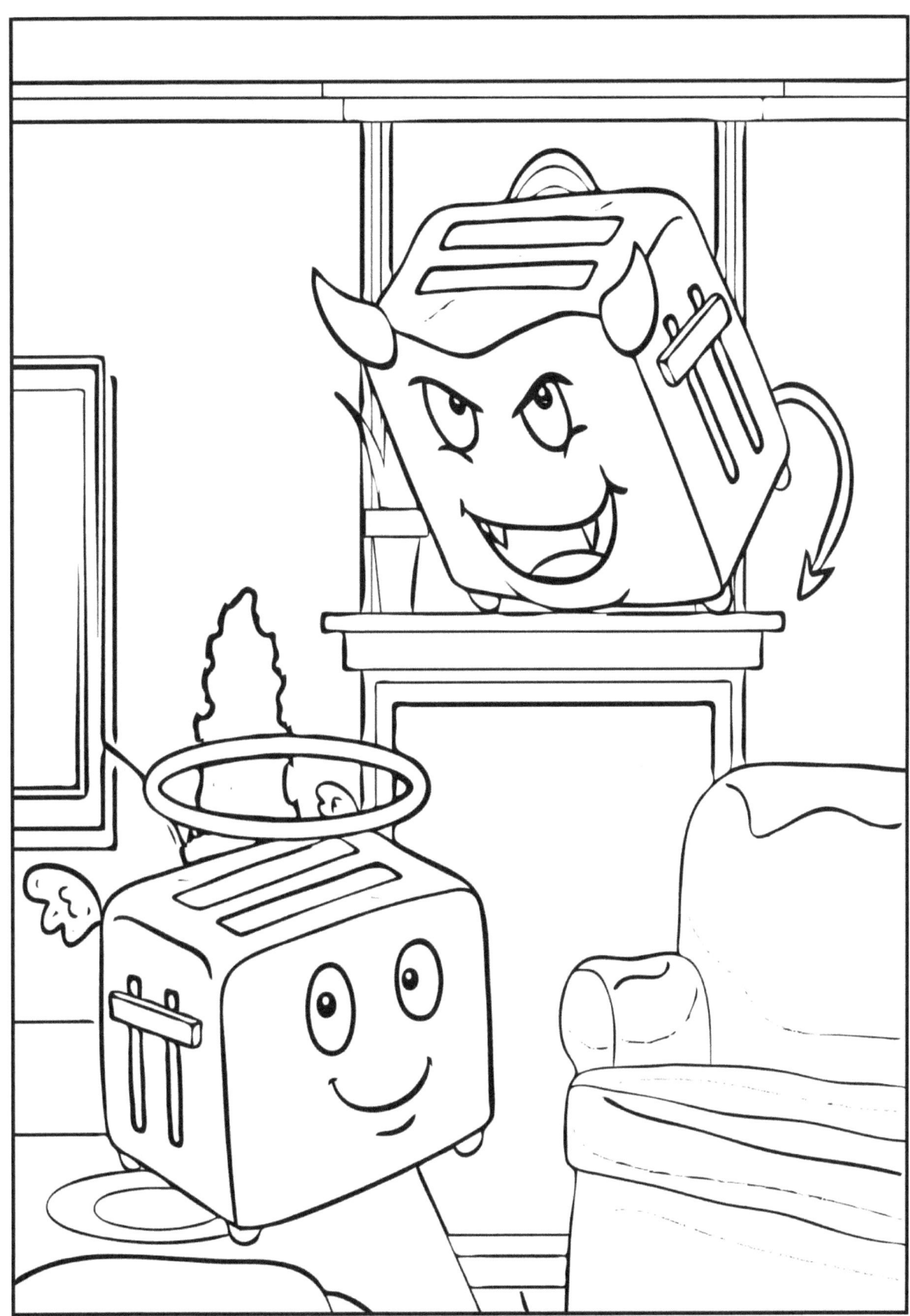

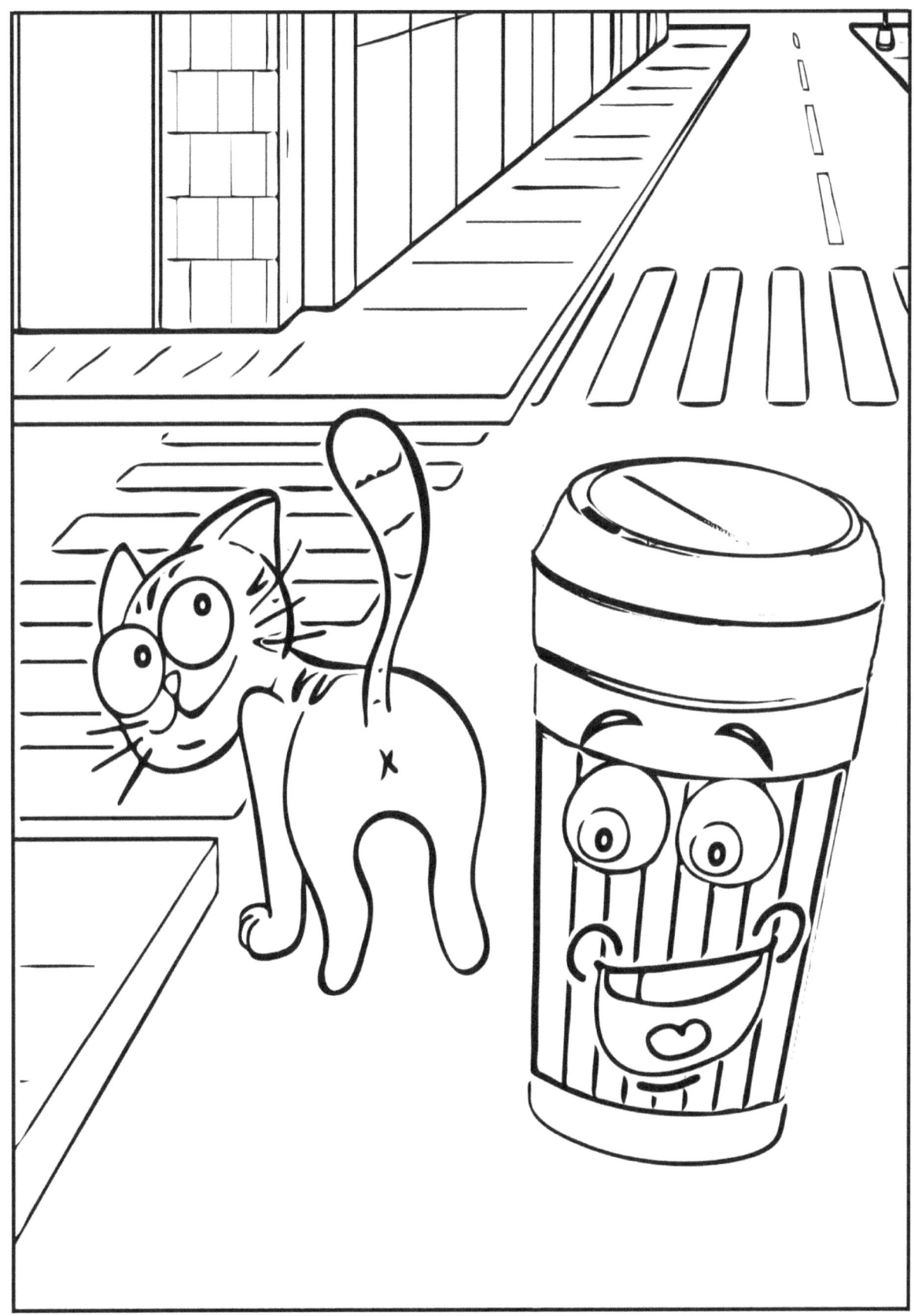

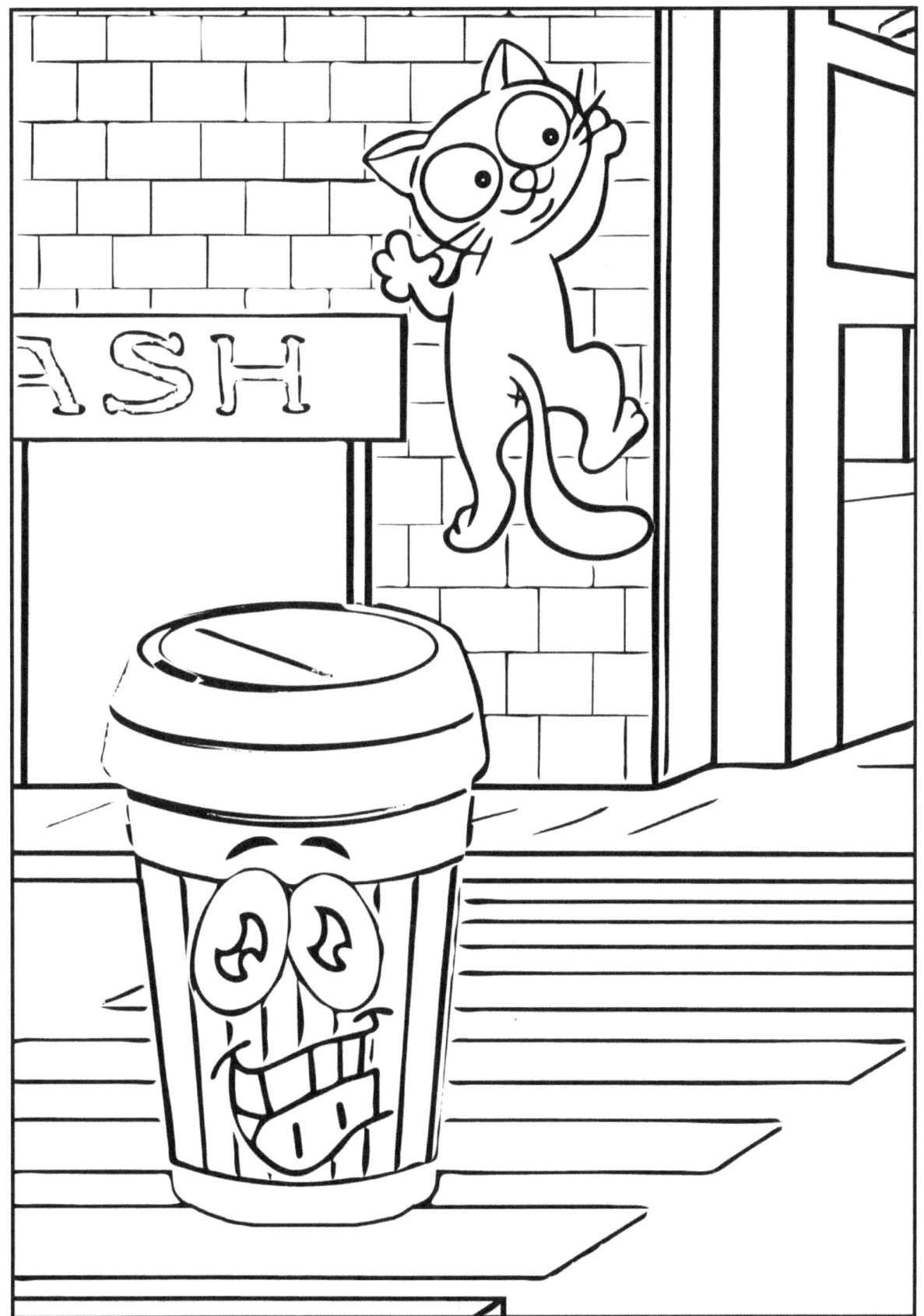

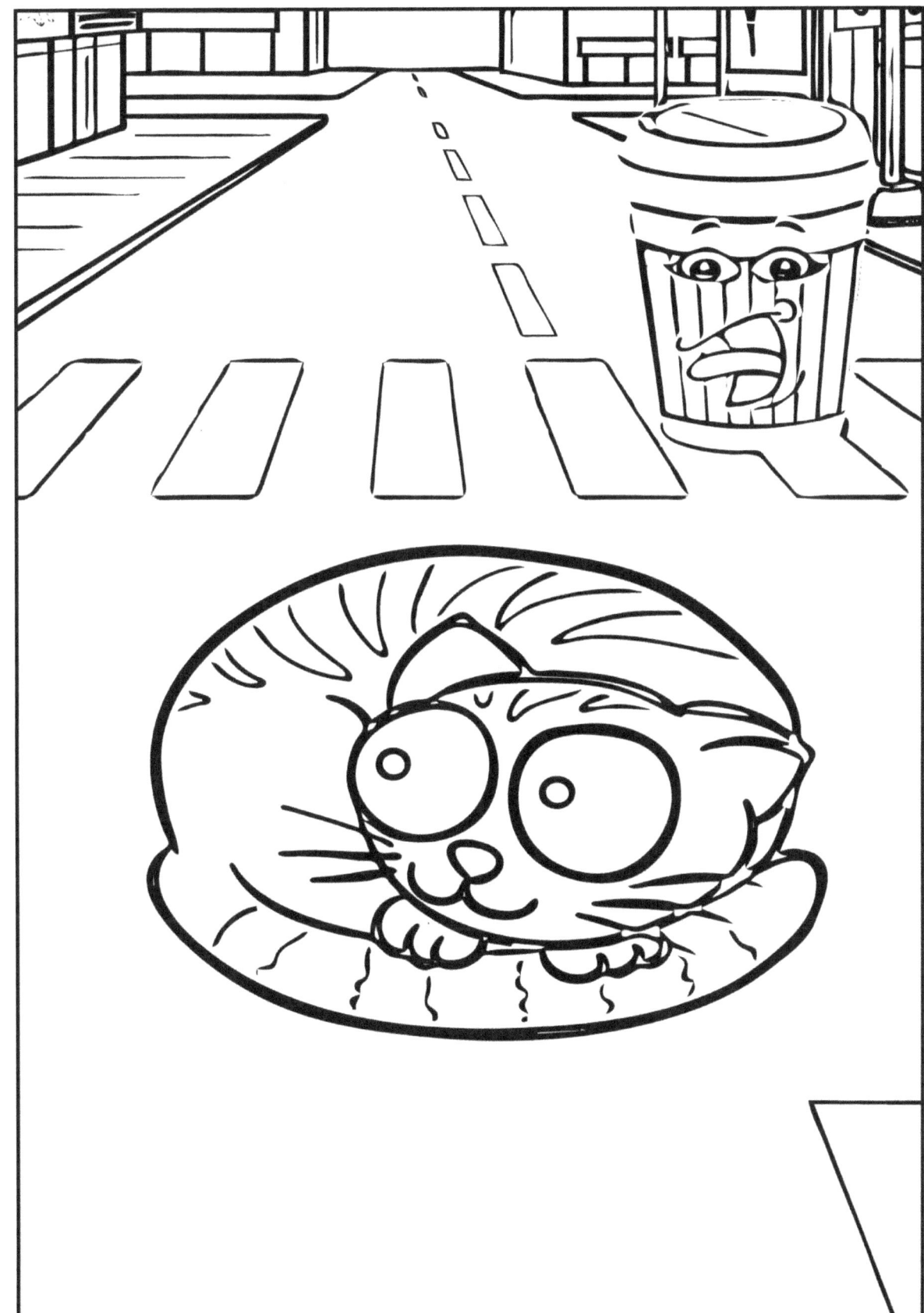

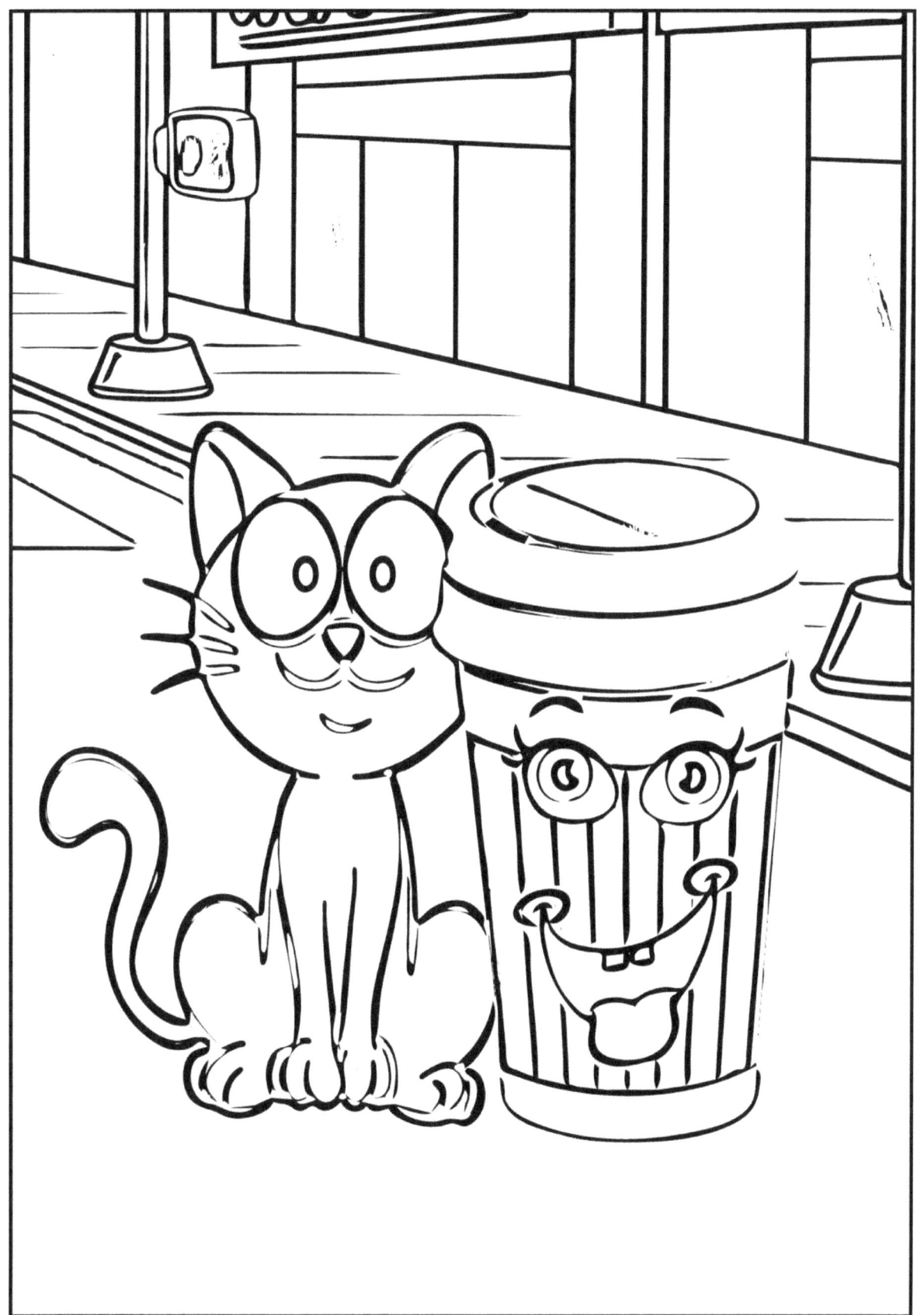

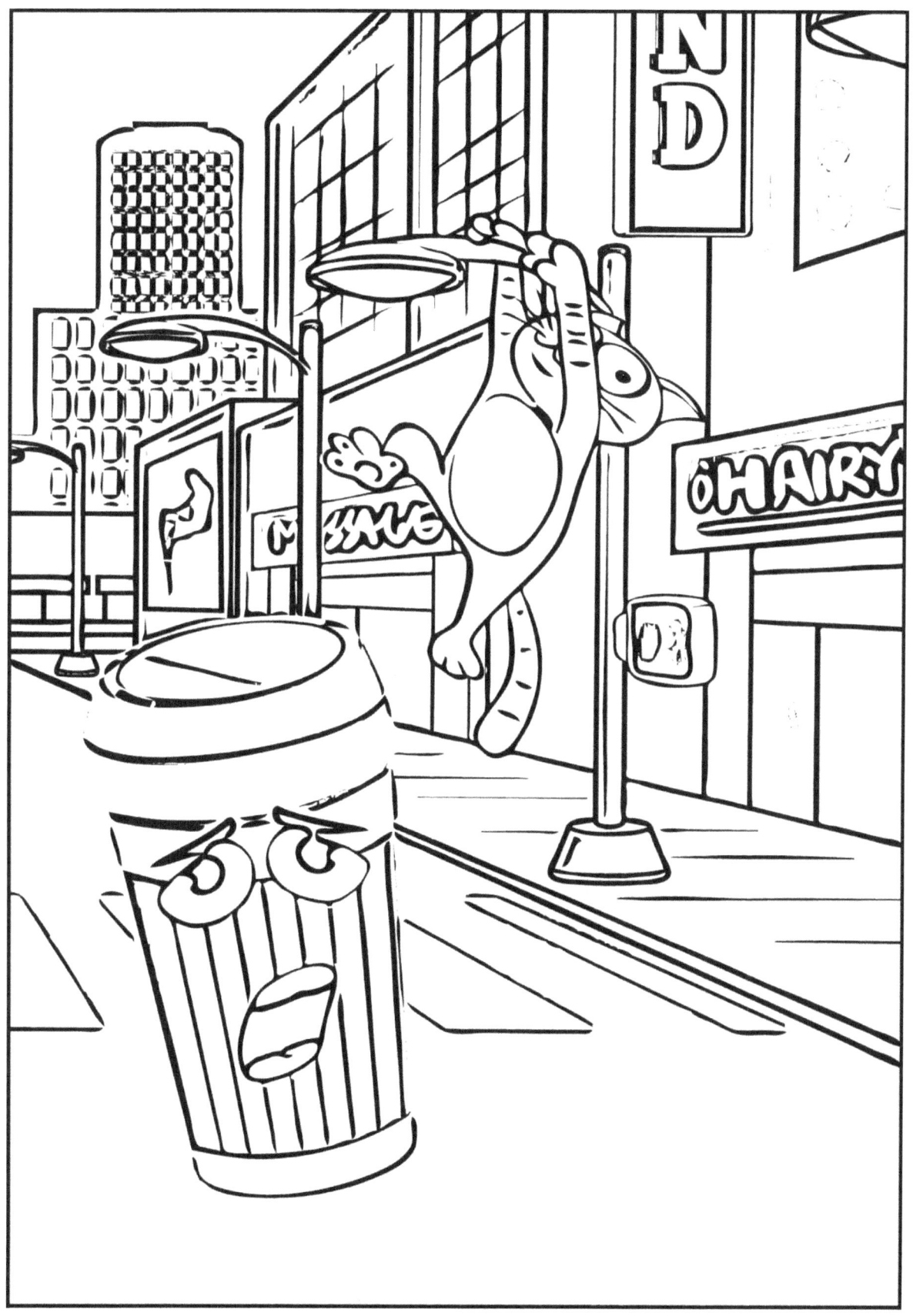

MYSTIC FOREST of CHI

Coloring Book For Adults

Fantasy Art Coloring Book For Stress Relief

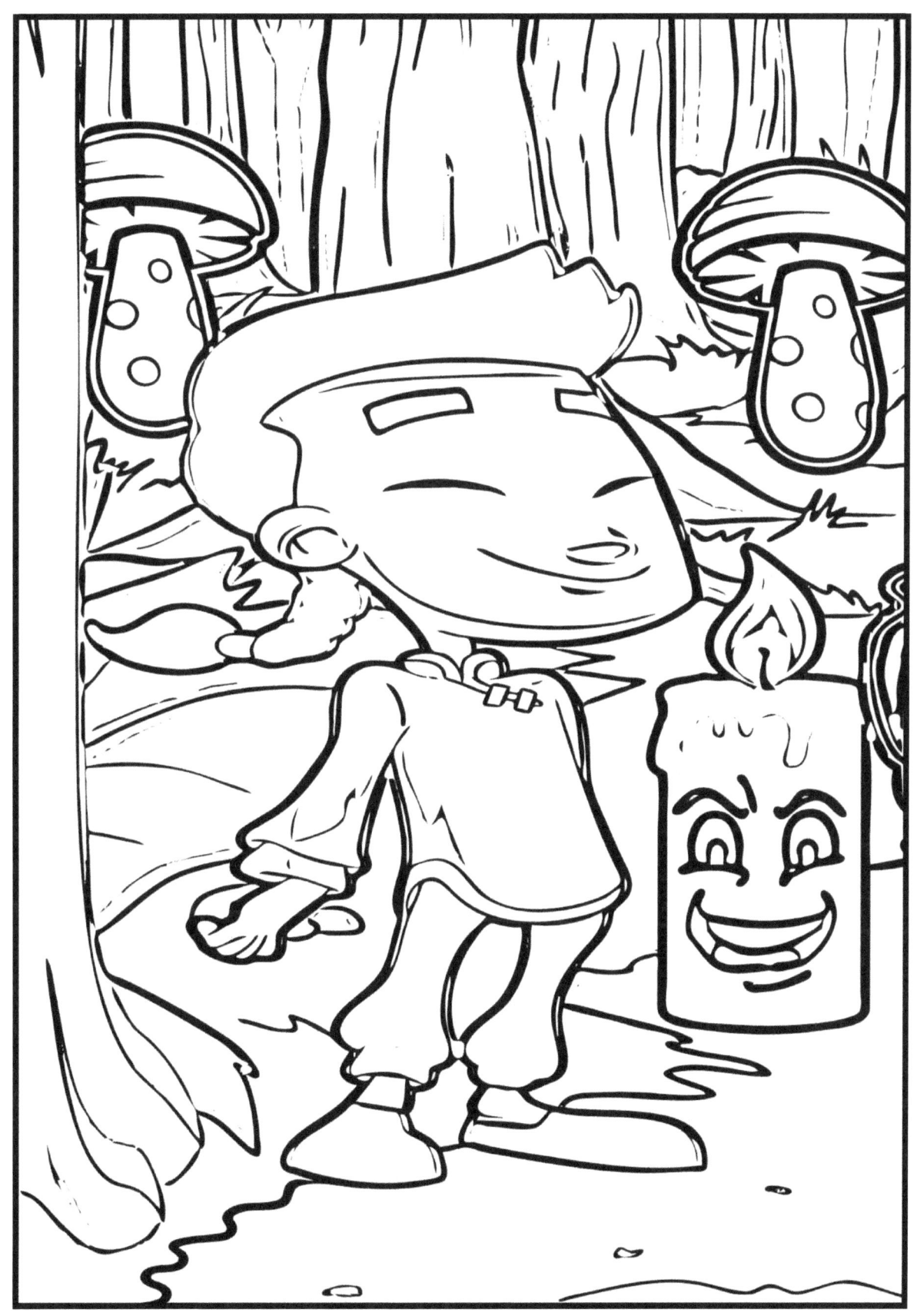

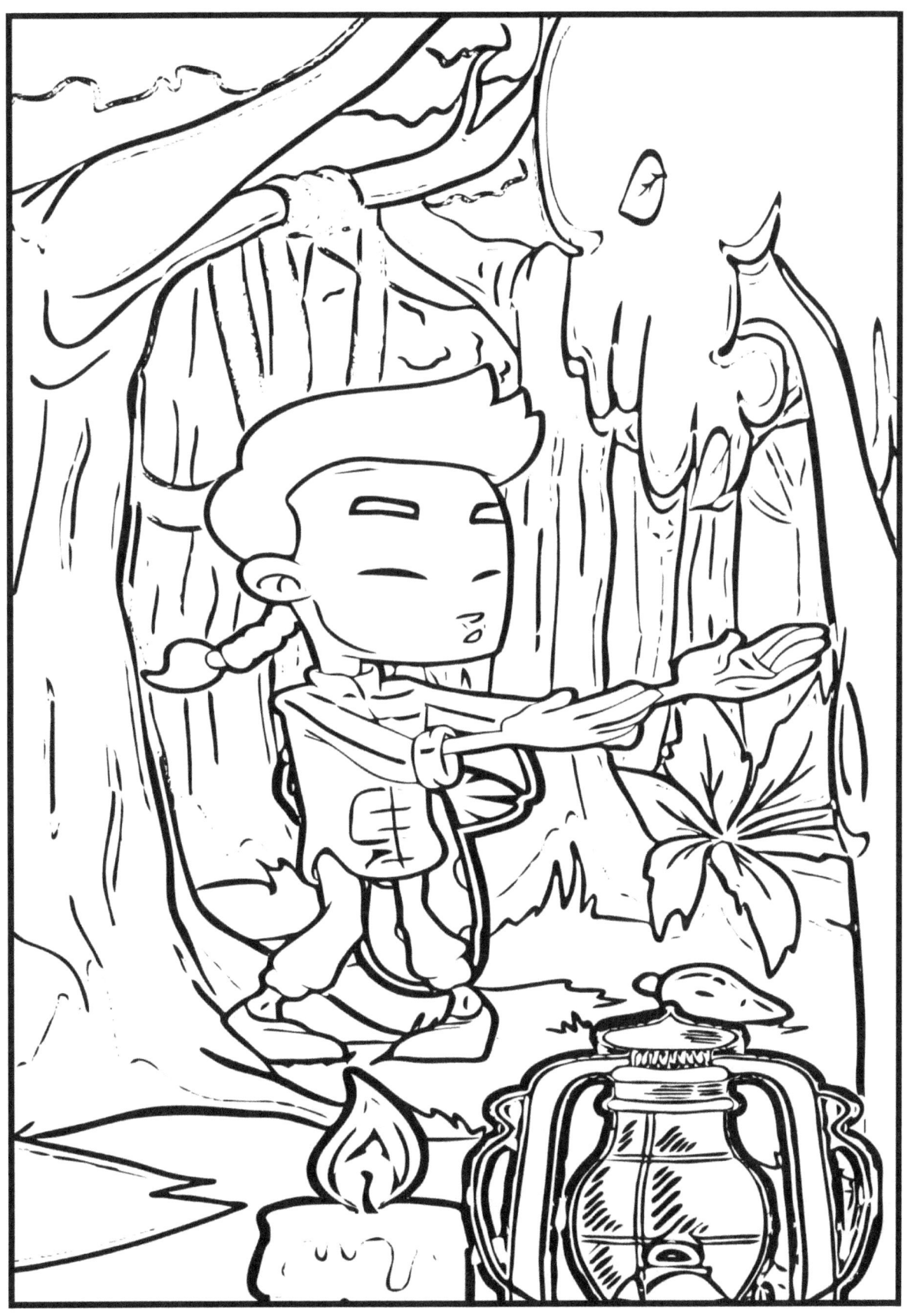

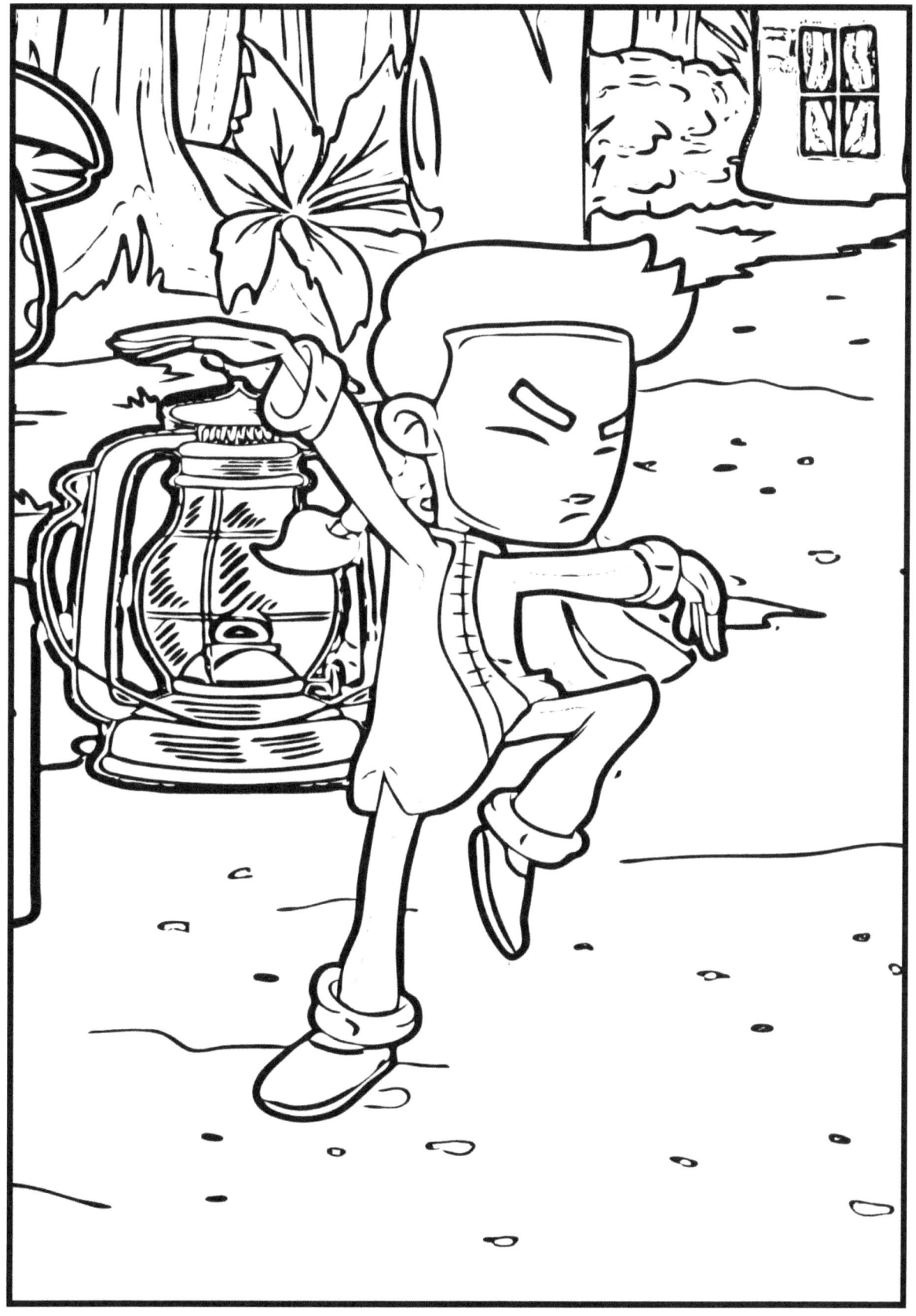

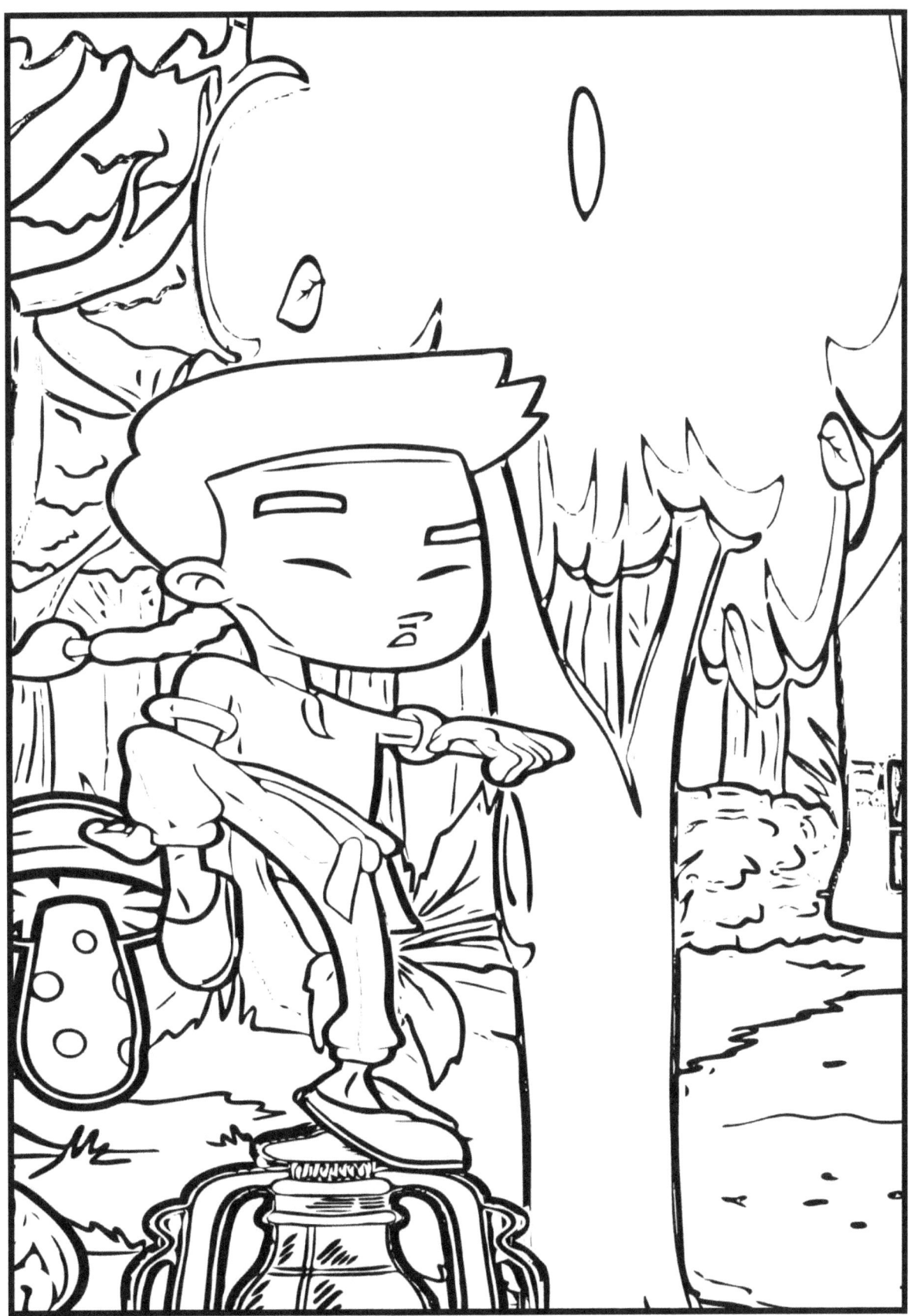

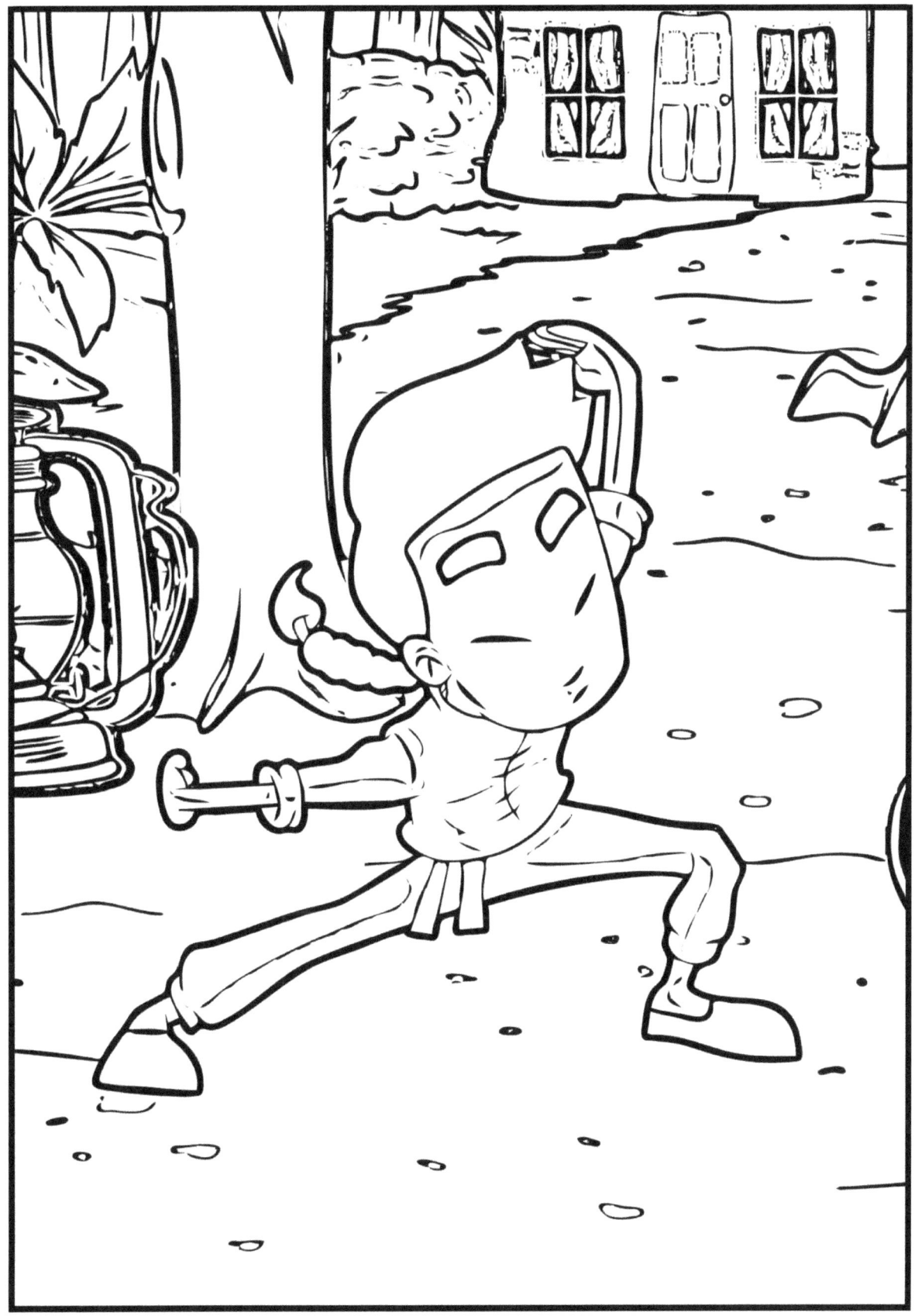

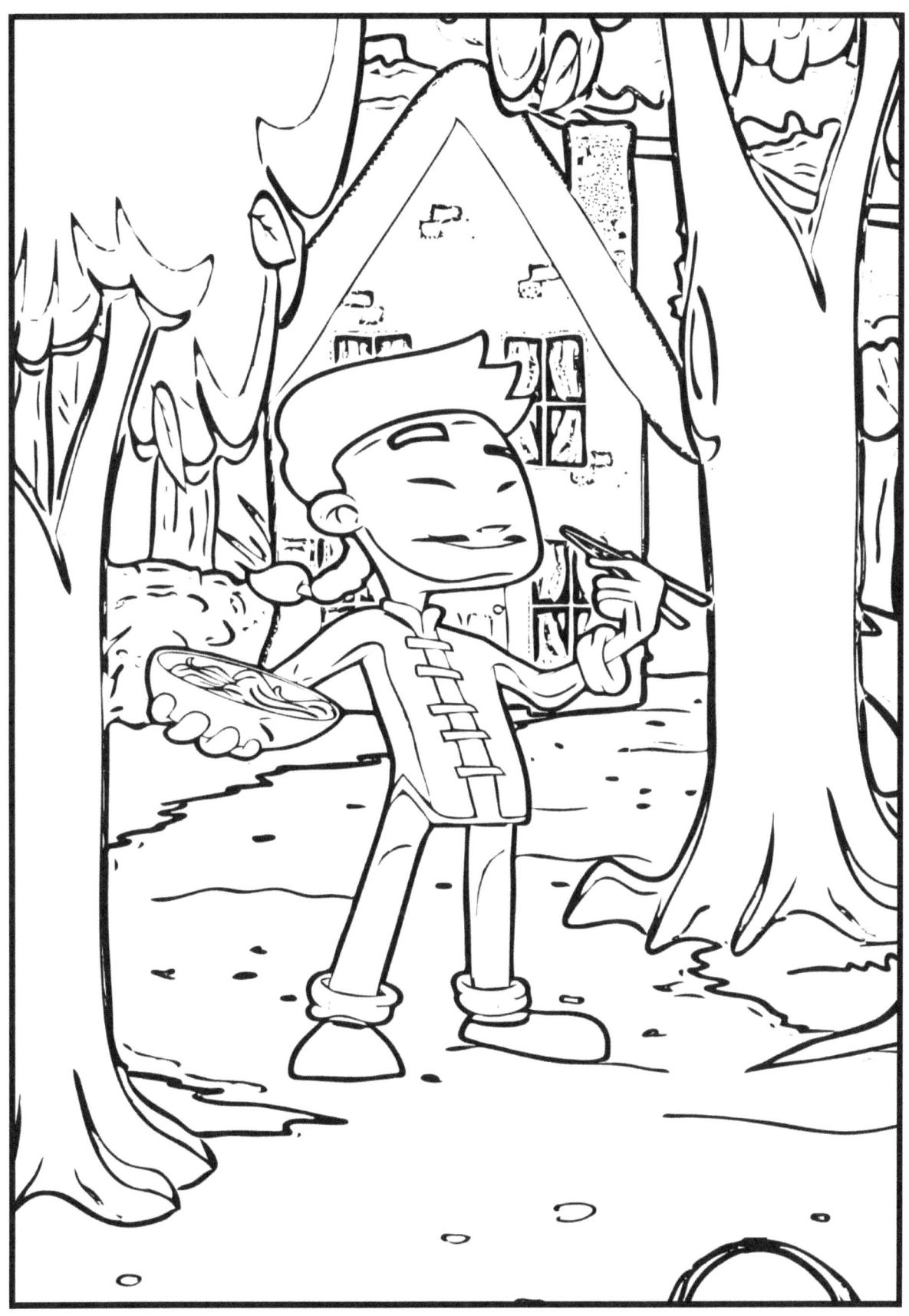

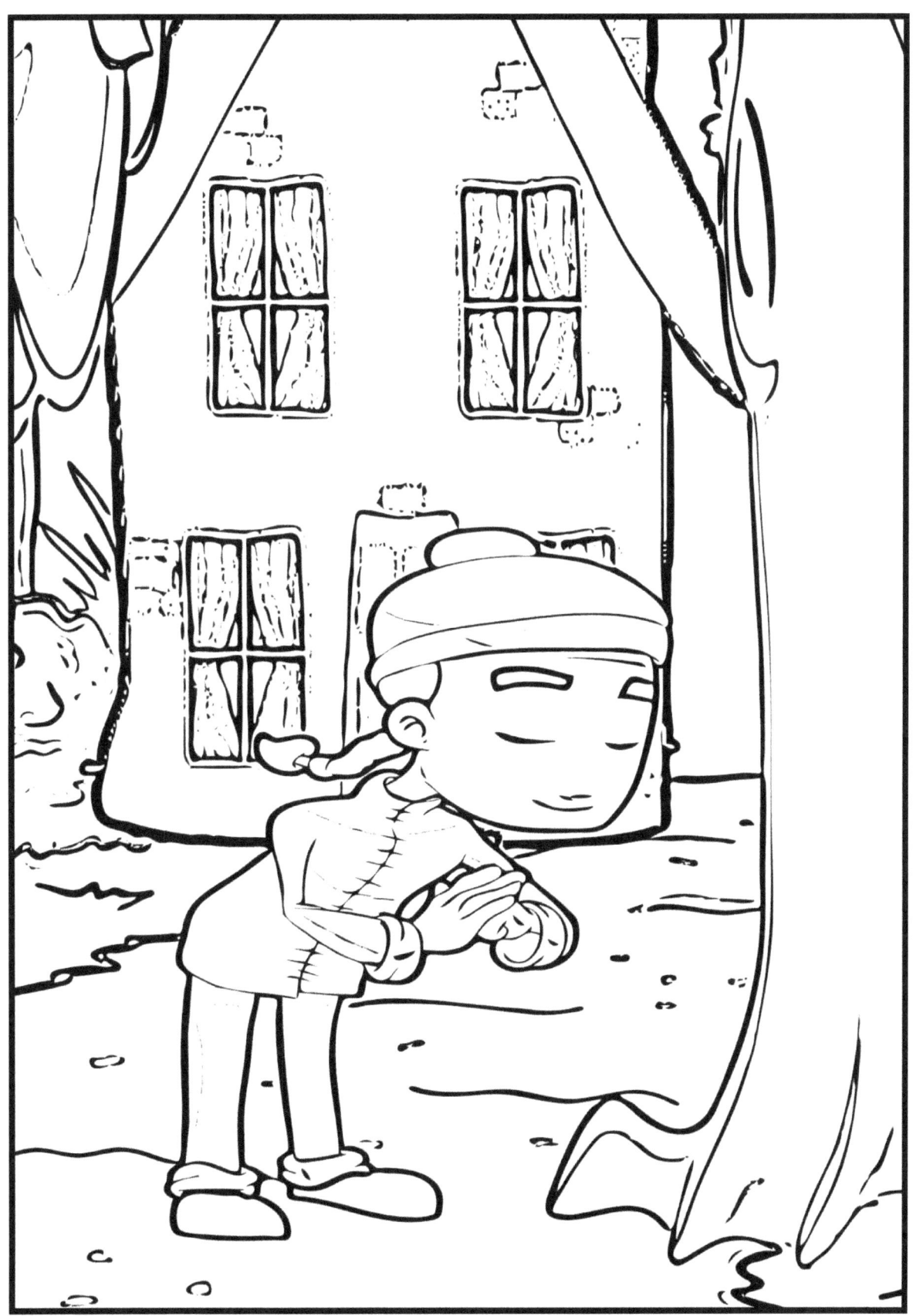

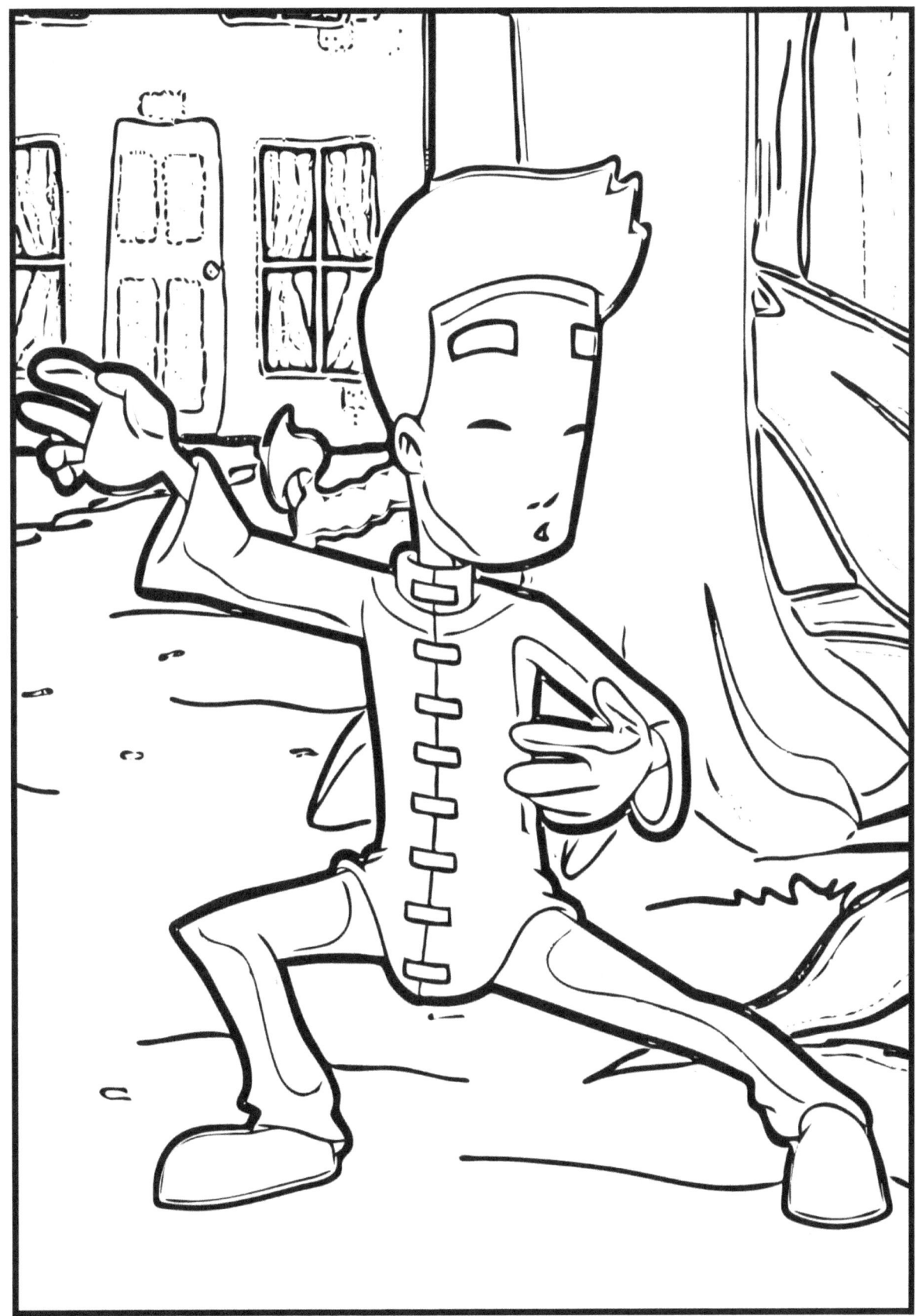

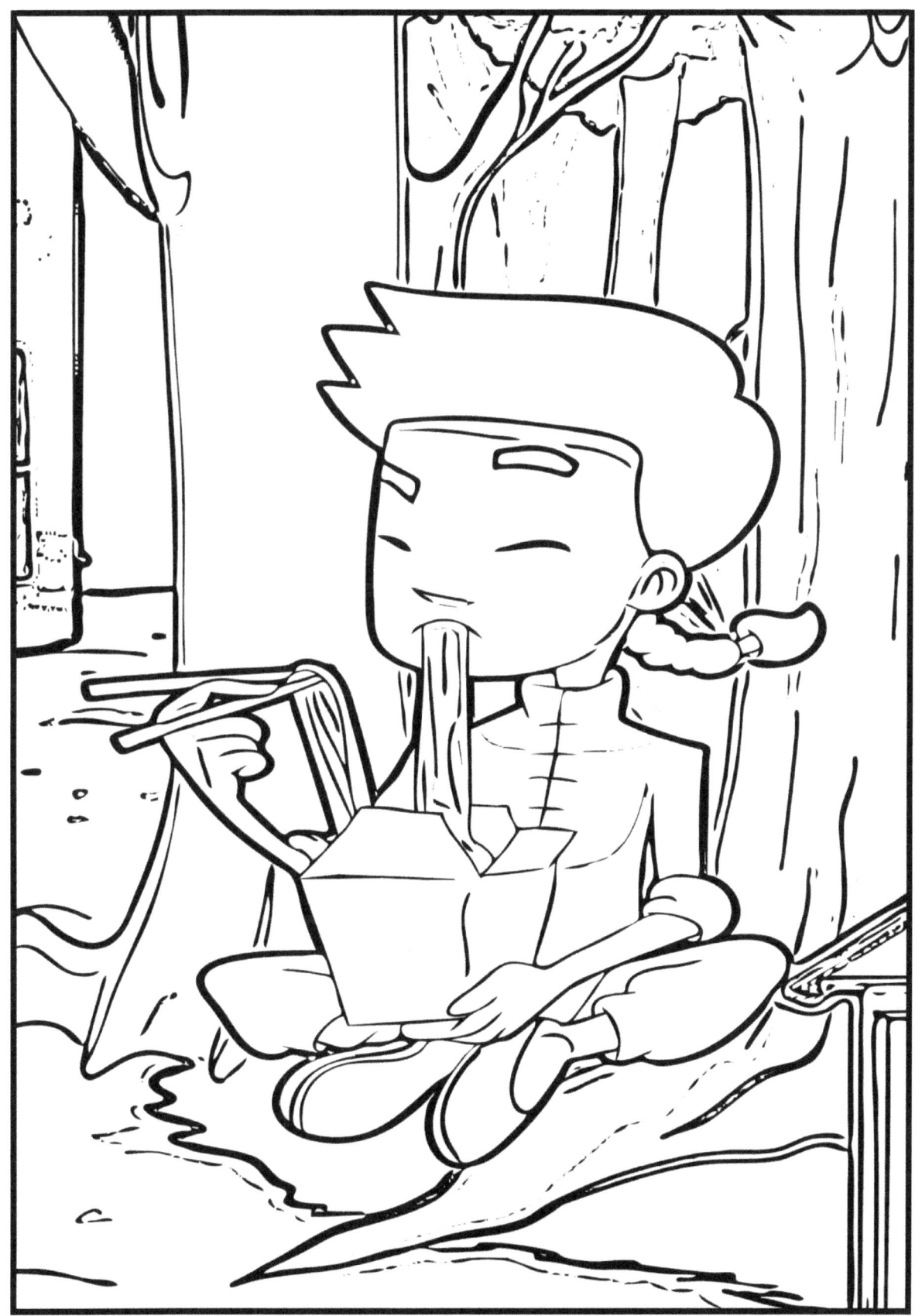

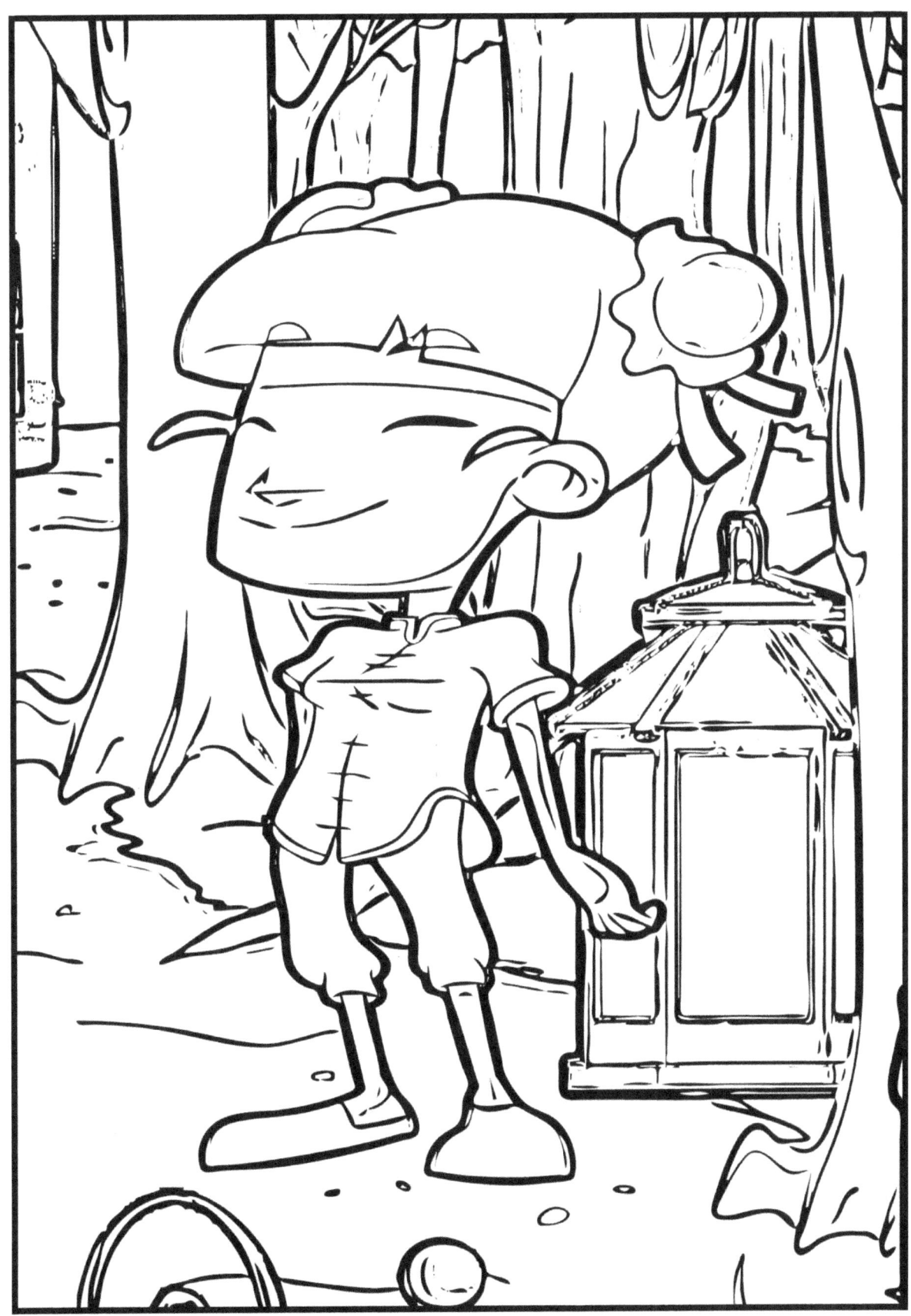

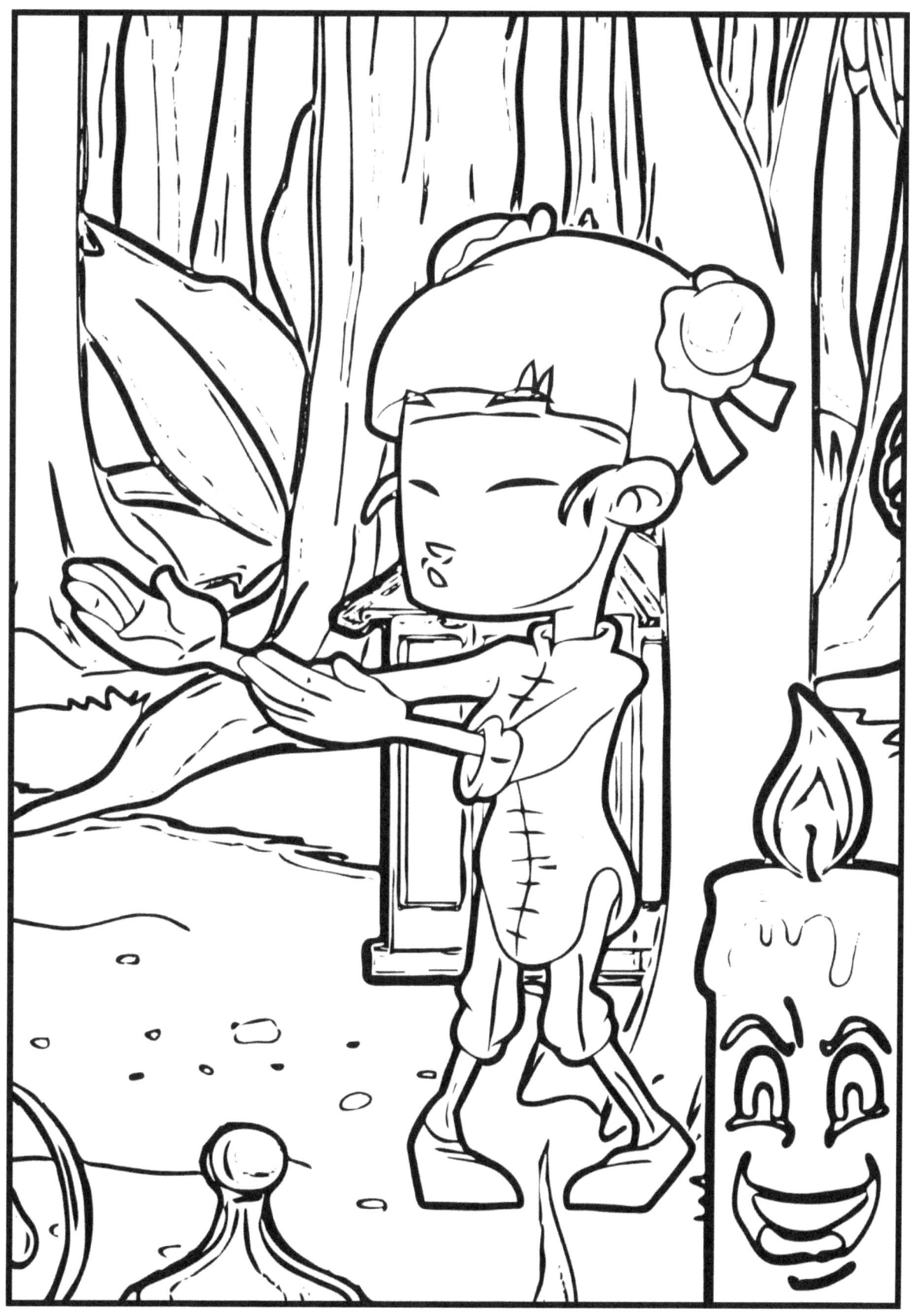

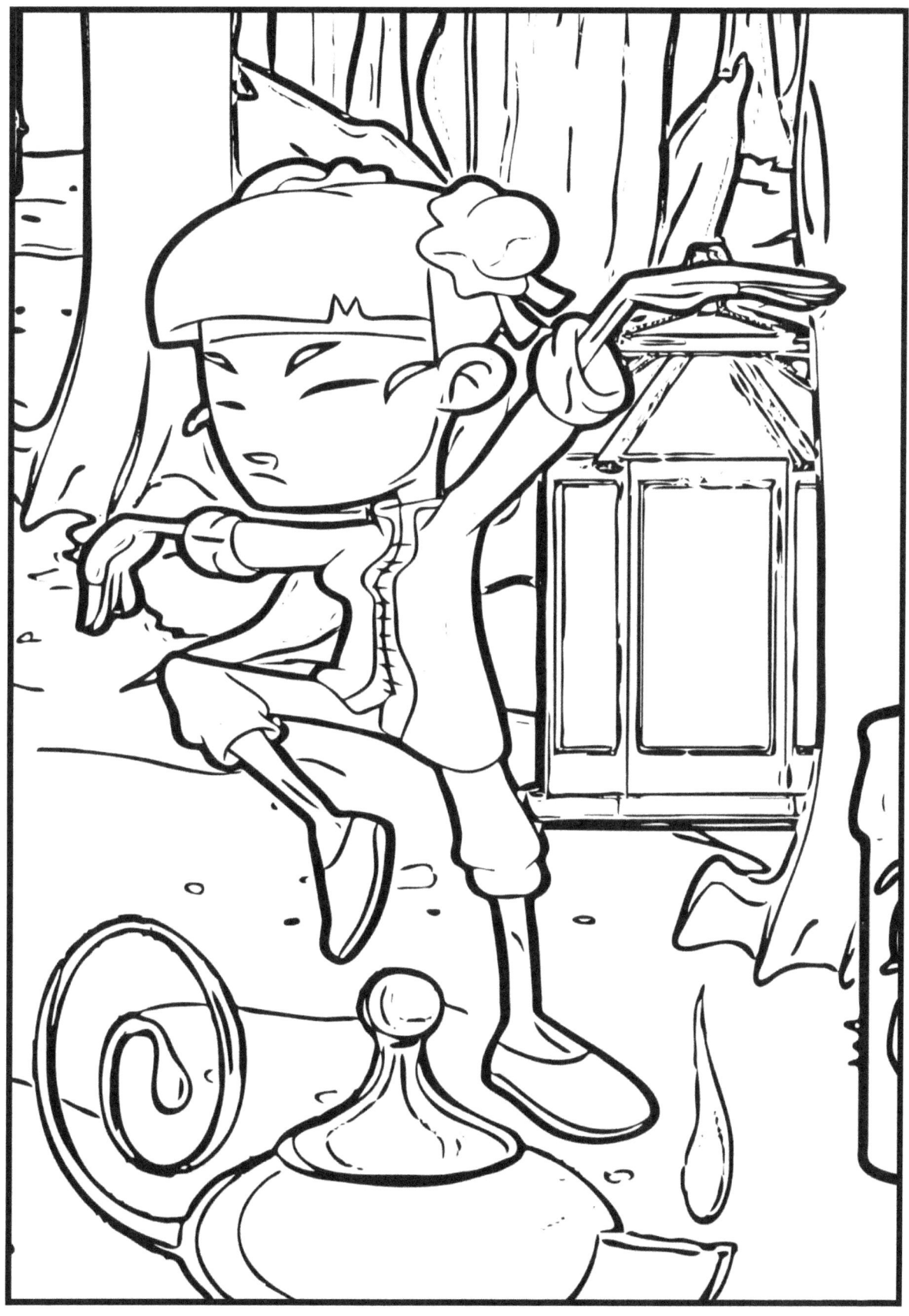

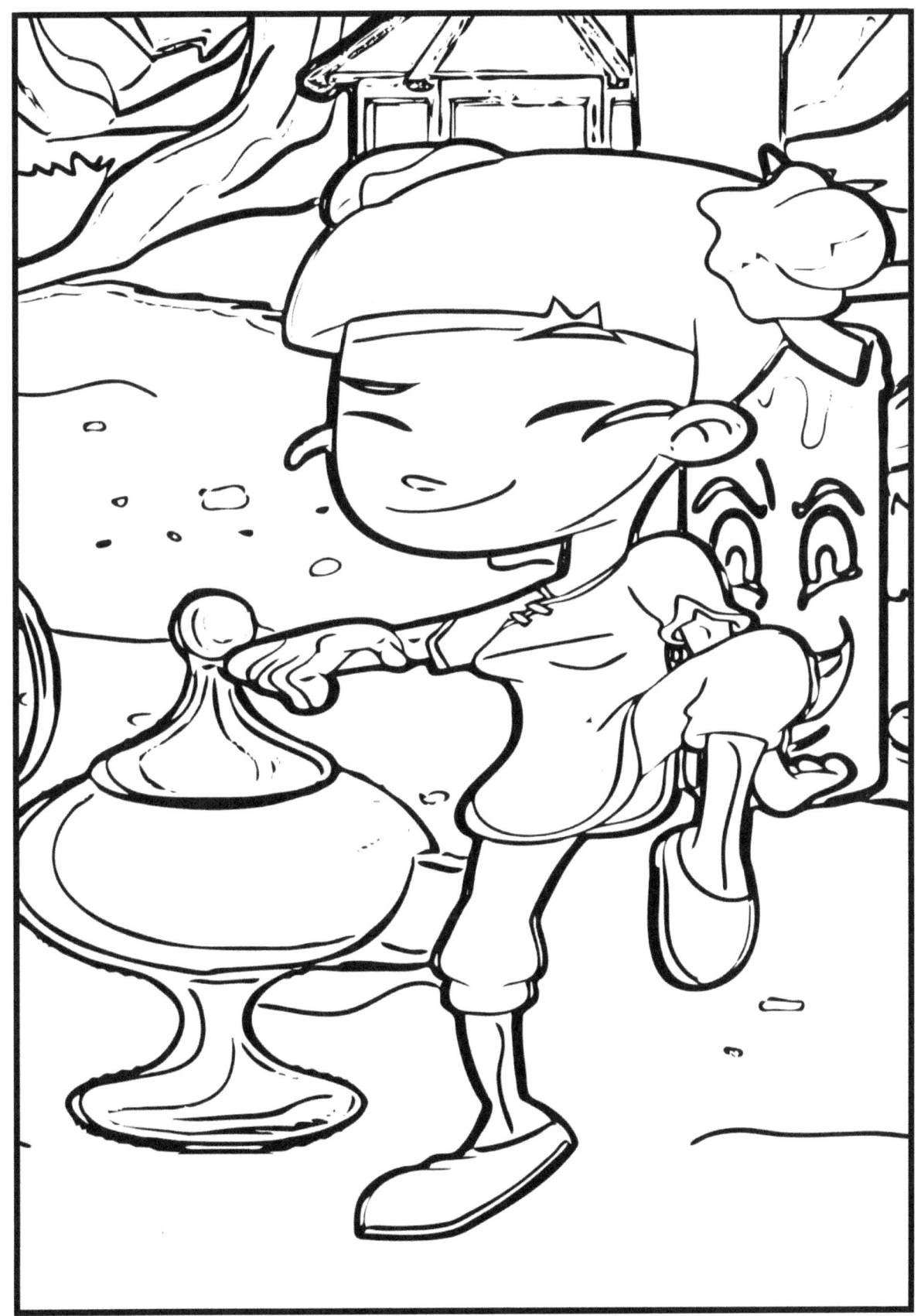

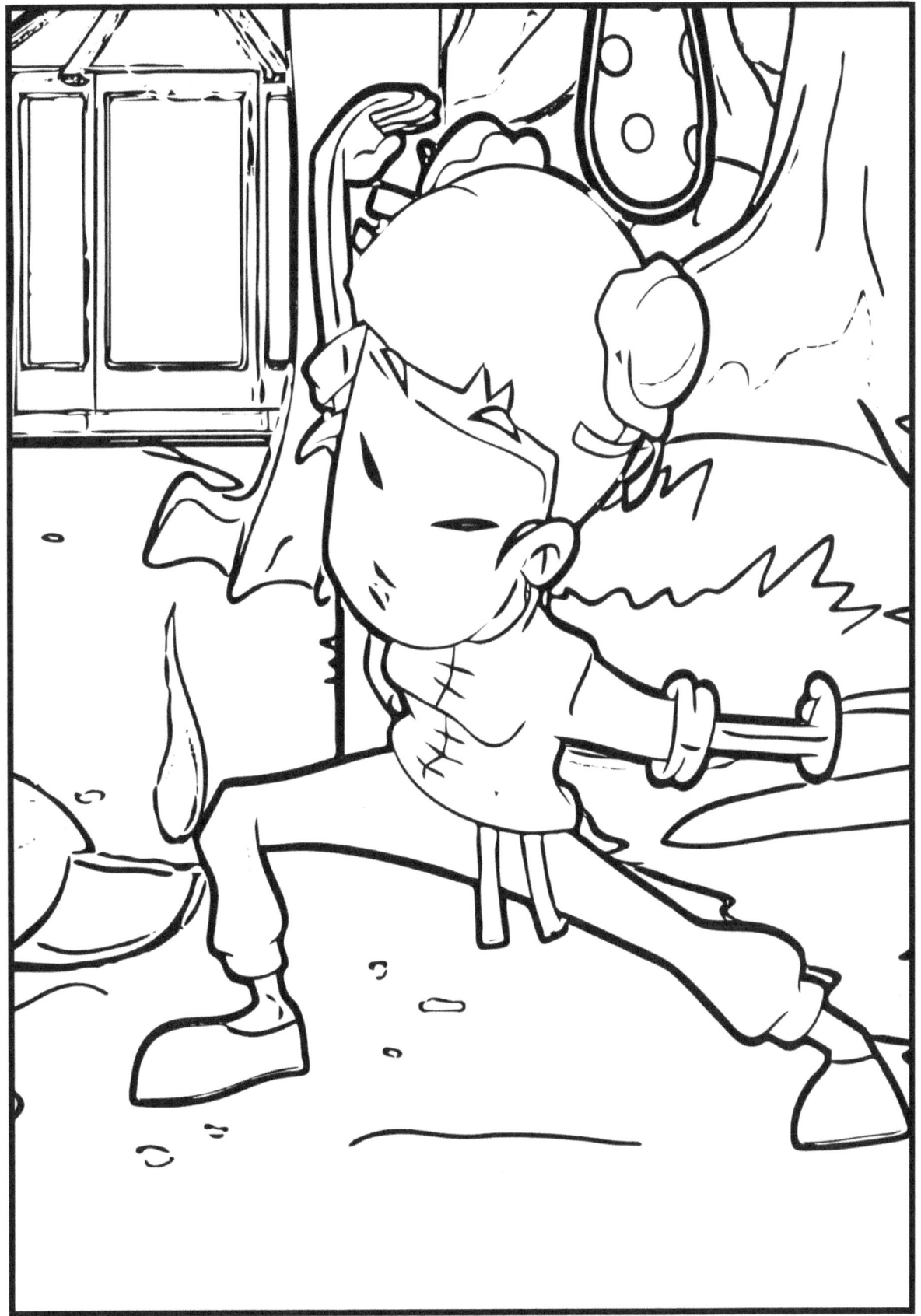

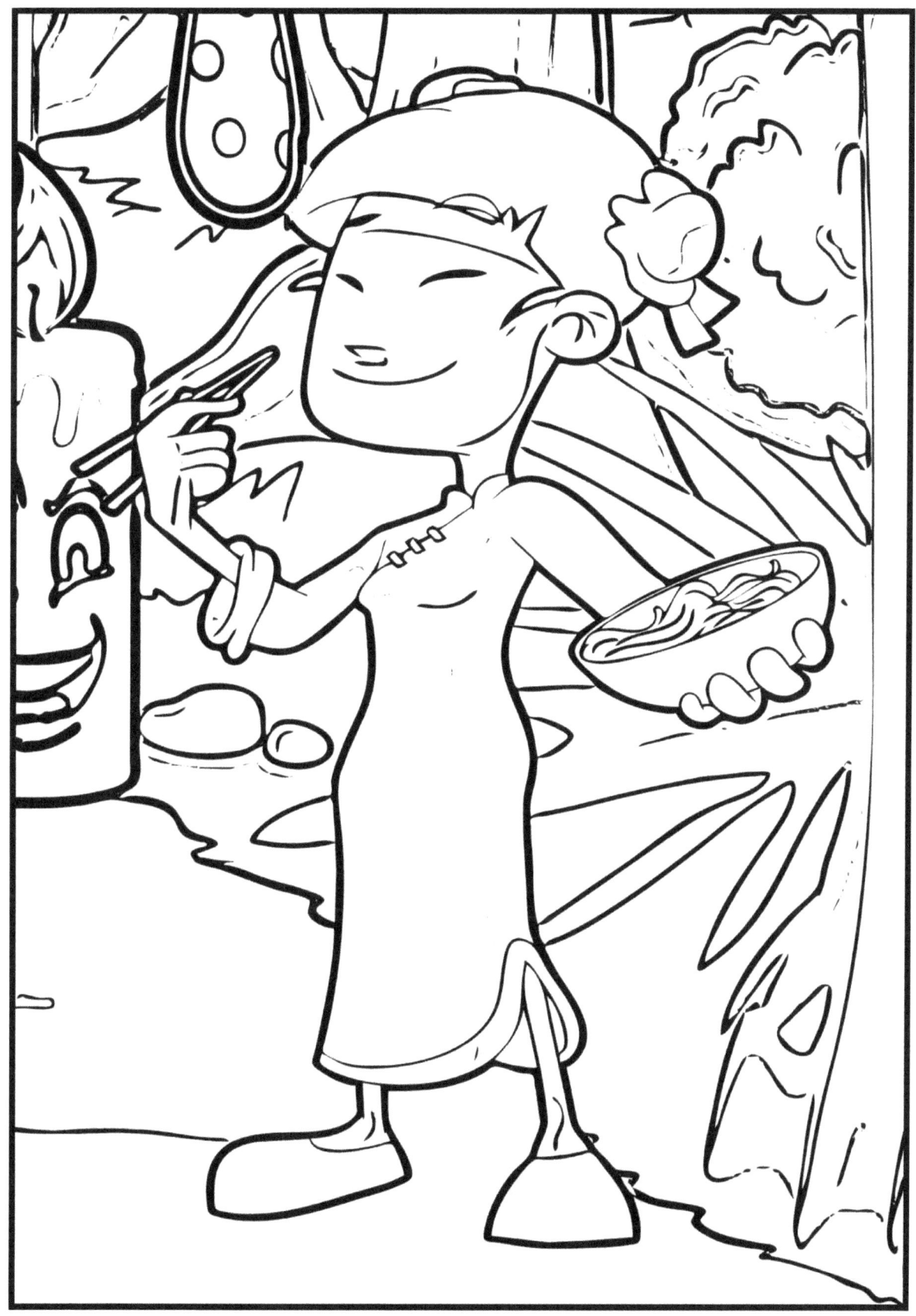

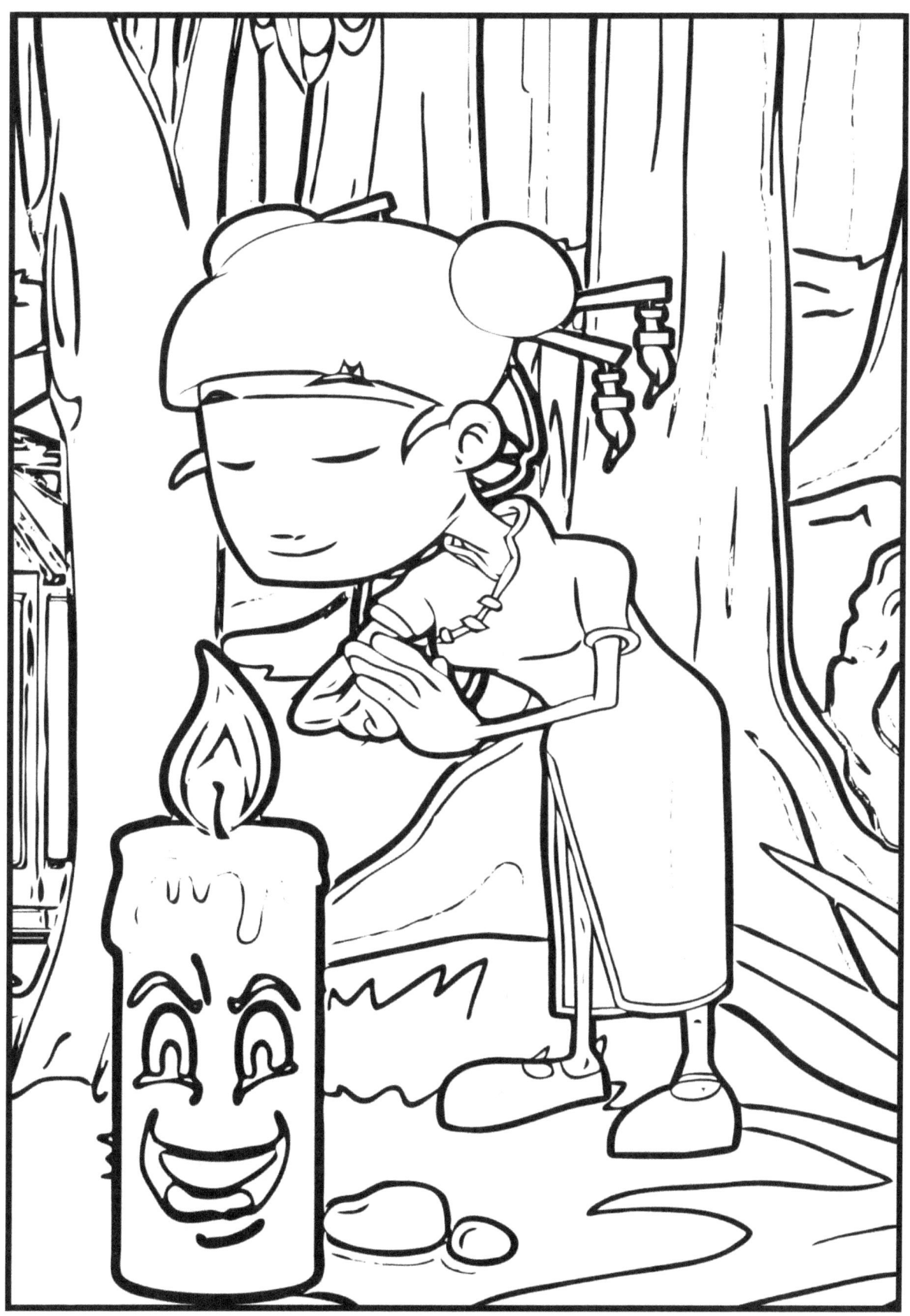

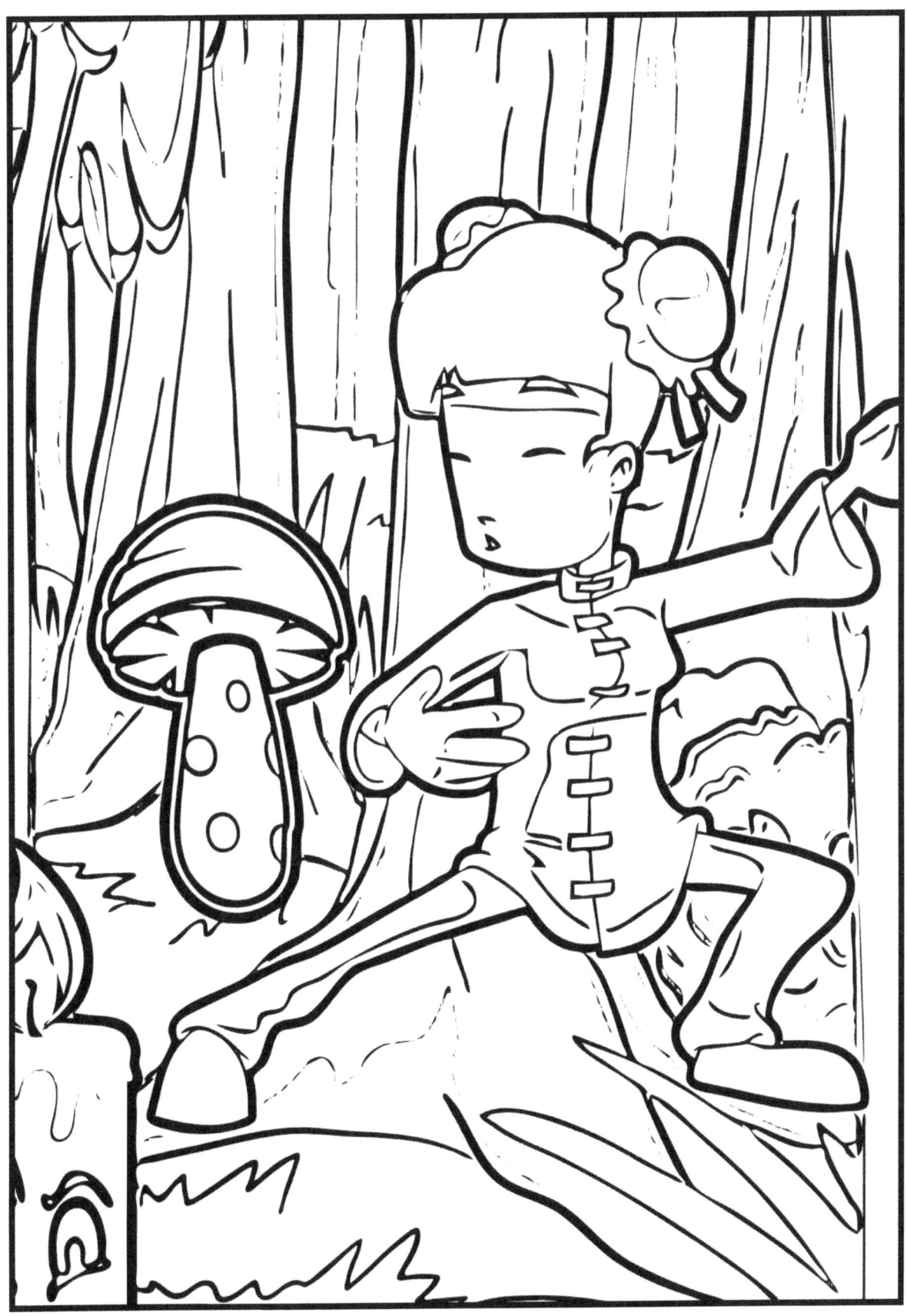

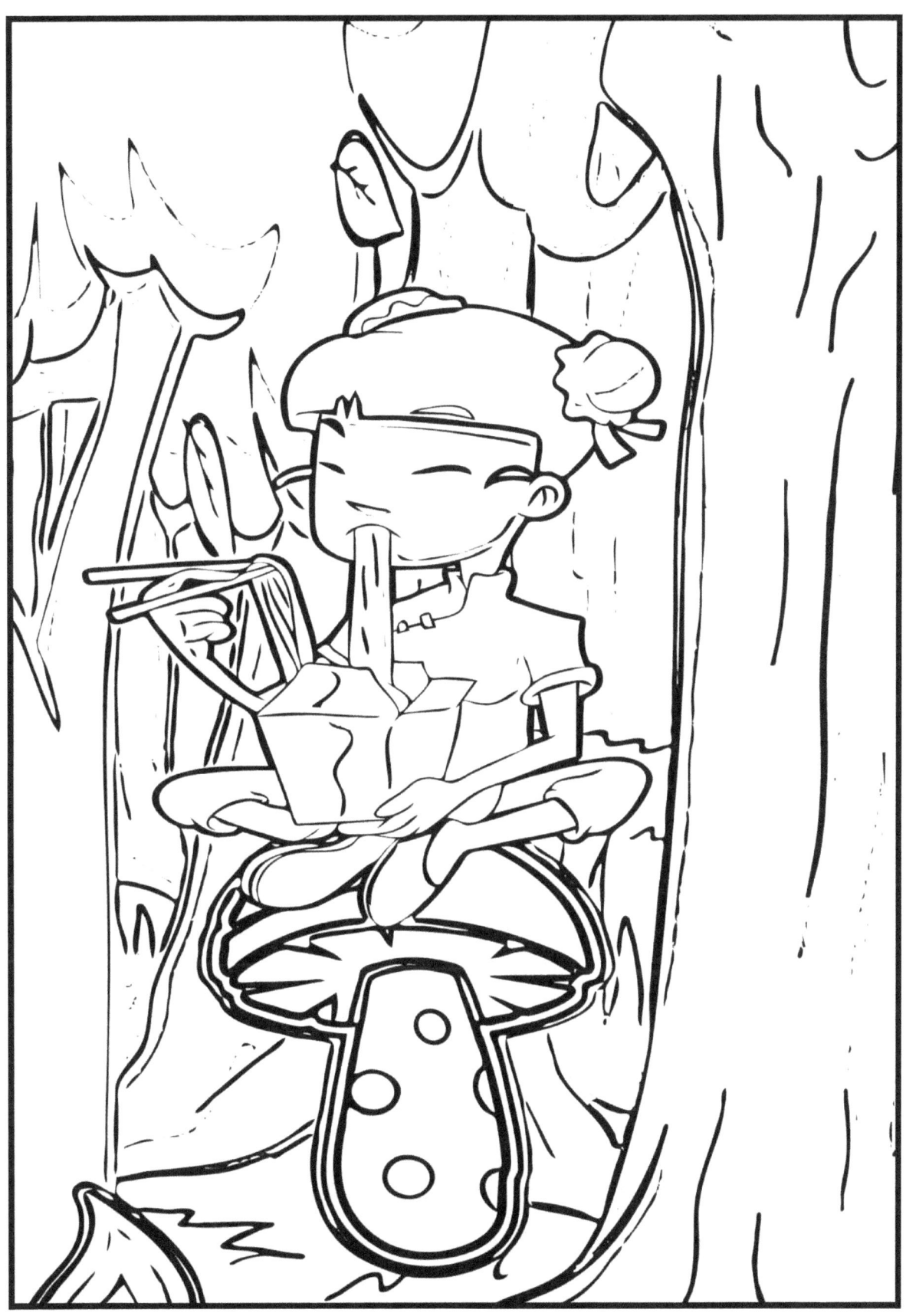